Dadlands

DADLANDS

the alternative handbook for new fathers

Daniel Blythe

CAPSTONE

Published in 2006 by Capstone Publishing Ltd (A Wiley Company), The Atrium, Southern Gate, Chichester, West Sussex, PO19 8SQ, England. Phone (+44) 1243 779777

Email (for orders and customer service enquires): cs-books@wiley.co.uk
Visit our Home Page on www.wiley.co.uk or www.wiley.com

Other Wiley Editorial Offices
John Wiley & Sons, Inc. 111 River Street, Hoboken, NJ 07030, USA
Jossey-Bass, 989 Market Street, San Francisco, CA 94103–1741, USA
Wiley-VCH Verlag GmbH, Pappellaee 3, D-69469 Weinheim, Germany
John Wiley & Sons Australia, Ltd, 33 Park Road, Milton, Queensland, 4064, Australia
John Wiley & Sons (Asia) Pte Ltd, 2 Clementi Loop #02–01, Jin Xing Distripark, Singapore 129809
John Wiley & Sons Canada Ltd, 22 Worcester Road, Etobicoke, Ontario, Canada, M9W 1L1
Wiley also publishes its books in a variety of electronic formats. Some content that appears in print may not be available in electronic books.

British Library Cataloguing-in-Publication Data
A catalogue record for this book is available from the British Library

ISBN13   978-1-84112-679-1
ISBN10   1-84112-679-9

Typeset in Swiss 721 BT by Sparks (www.sparks.co.uk).
Printed and bound in Great Britain by TJ International Ltd, Padstow, Cornwall.
This book is printed on acid-free paper responsibly manufactured from sustainable forestry in which at least two trees are planted for each one used for paper production.
10 9 8 7 6 5 4 3 2 1

Dedicated with love to my children

Elinor and Samuel

who may recognize themselves occasionally

Contents

	Author's note	ix
Chapter 1	**Enjoy the Silence**	1
	The calm before the storm	
Chapter 2	**The Kick Inside**	4
	Baby is here, and it's going to be personal	
Chapter 3	**Possibly Maybe**	6
	The 'are you emotionally ready?' quiz	
Chapter 4	**Everybody's Changing**	10
	Your flexible antenatal preparation course, just for dads	
Chapter 5	**Treat Her Like a Lady**	14
	Life around a pregnant woman	
Chapter 6	**Do You Really Want to Hurt Me?**	21
	Labour: if it isn't hurting, it isn't working …	
Chapter 7	**World Shut Your Mouth**	27
	Unsolicited advice and where to shove it	
Chapter 8	**Boulevard of Broken Dreams**	33
	Things you can no longer do. It's scary	
Chapter 9	**Don't Call Me Baby**	37
	You need to find a name for this thing	
Chapter 10	**Nothing Can Stop Us**	41
	The one-week expert	
Chapter 11	**One Cool Remove**	43
	More bodily fluids than you ever thought possible	
Chapter 12	**She Drives Me Crazy**	49
	You can leave the house	
Chapter 13	**Take Me Out**	55
	Trying to get away, into the night	
Chapter 14	**Pump Up the Volume**	63
	What a pair of lungs	
Chapter 15	**Pacific State**	69
	Parenting for dummies	
Chapter 16	**Eat to the Beat**	72
	The mysteries of baby 'food'	
Chapter 17	**Moving On Up**	78
	Look out … he's starting to crawl	
Chapter 18	**Walking On Sunshine**	81
	And now he's upright and dangerous	
Chapter 19	**What Have I Done to Deserve This?**	85
	Our simple toddler quiz	

Chapter 20	**Semi-detached Suburban Mr James**	88
	Some people you may not like to meet	
Chapter 21	**See Emily Play**	92
	The joys of toys	
Chapter 22	**Don't Look Back in Anger**	97
	Can you remember when it was all fields? The perils of nostalgia	
Chapter 23	**Money's Too Tight to Mention**	101
	But we'll mention it anyway	
Chapter 24	**If You Tolerate This, Your Children Will Be Next**	108
	Germs, Calpol and daytime TV	
Chapter 25	**It's the End of the World As We Know It (And I Feel Fine)**	112
	When work intervenes	
Chapter 26	**Say Hello, Wave Goodbye**	119
	Childcare: it's not a sin	
Chapter 27	**Wonderful Life**	126
	Some salutary tales	
Chapter 28	**There She Goes**	131
	Tantrums and tears	
Chapter 29	**Blue Monday**	135
	Wash your mouth out	
Chapter 30	**People Get Real**	138
	Mess management	
Chapter 31	**I Predict a Riot**	143
	Party games, with optional frontiers	
Chapter 32	**Zeroes and Ones**	151
	Education, stimulation, appreciation	
Chapter 33	**Word Up**	154
	Reading, writing and arithmetic	
Chapter 34	**Kill Your Television**	159
	Why don't you … meet TV halfway?	
Chapter 35	**Would I Lie to You?**	166
	Santa Claus, and other fictions you have to share	
Chapter 36	**Solitude Standing**	172
	Me-time	
Chapter 37	**A Design For Life**	175
	We reach Reception class with a spring in our step … don't we?	
Chapter 38	**I Wanna Be a Winner**	182
	Medals for everyone: why it doesn't work	
Chapter 39	**Alphabet Street**	187
	A final A–Z of parenting	
Chapter 40	**There Is a Light that Never Goes Out**	194
	The good parent	
Appendix 1	**Is There Something I Should Know?**	199
Appendix 2	**Like a Child Again**	202
Afterword	**Put the Message in the Box**	206

Author's note

There is something vaguely disparaging about calling children 'it'. The pronoun makes me uneasy, even when it's used with the best of intentions.

So what I've done throughout this book is to use 'he' and 'she' (or 'him' and 'her') fairly indiscriminately, to reflect the fact that some of you will have girl babies and some will have boys. I have one of each, so it seemed logical. I hope this keeps everyone happy, and that nobody decides to count up all the pronouns and tell me that I have more of one than of the other. Enjoy this even-handedness, as it's about the only piece of political correctness you'll find within these pages.

DB

Chapter 1
Enjoy the Silence

You can't find out how to be a good parent by reading books, so this book doesn't even pretend to be a parenting guide. There are plenty of those out there already, written with honourable intent and put together by people with far more impressive qualifications than mine. Lots of them seem to treat parenthood like some sort of qualification which requires you to self-assess on a continuous basis. You tick whereabouts on the continuum you are, to show that you are working to the prescribed Learning Outcomes in your Modules: 'Get baby to sleep by feeding: Competent, Not Yet Competent or Working Towards?'

Well, relax. This book isn't like that. It's about what it's *really* like to be a father – the good, the bad, the ugly (of course, nobody's baby is ugly) and the messy.

You see, here's a funny thing. Women talk about their kids all the time. They do it at work, over coffee, over meals, over breastfeeding, at baby and toddler groups, at school and nursery gates, on the phone and on mums' Internet forums. Men, on the other hand, still sometimes seem to feel they can't. Maybe we'd like to, but in the end it's safer and less boring for everyone if we chat about the holes in the national team defence, the new Coldplay album or the precise measurements of Sarah Michelle Gellar.

All of which is fine – but it does mean that, whether by choice or not, men don't always create the same support networks for talking about their children. Even on the Internet, there are far more forums for mums to chat than for dads, and even those which are nominally open to parents of either gender seem to attract more women participants.

It's sometimes argued that this is because we compartmen-talize – we are used to having a drawer in our filing cabinet marked 'Baby', just before 'Bank'. That may be true, or it may be another of those sexual stereotypes – one of those generali-zations which you can't get away with throwing at women but which, for men, seem fair game.

As a man, I bet you're also not really bothered about whether other people choose to have children or not. You won't pity them, envy them, look down or up or even across to them. Your life and theirs will probably not intersect very much from now on anyway. While women are sniping at each other in the press all the time for their choice in the matter, it's not something men get terribly hot under the collar about. I wonder why? Is it because we are not so genetically encoded, or we don't hear the biologi-cal clock ticking (you can still become a dad in your seventies in theory), or that we simply don't define our power and status in terms of our position as dads and non-dads?

Walking in my shoes
Think of this book as a friend. It will take you down to the pub when your children have left you shell-shocked, puzzled, exhausted or unable to cope. It will sit you down, buy you a beer and talk to you. It will help you see the fun side of being a parent. It will reassure you that you are by no means the first to have blanched at the thought of attending a birth, to face the frustrations of a collapsing pushchair or to wonder which way round a nappy goes.

You'll find out that it's quite normal to be baffled by the range of baby foods on offer, and to be bemused by the odd conventions of Mum & Toddler groups. You're not alone in wondering if your child is watching too much television, or in being driven mad by the little one's incessant screaming.

We'll take you, in manageable chunks, from the first appearance of your gunky, bawling little person to the day you deliver a well-scrubbed, well-balanced child to the gate of the infants' school. You'll get the odd bit of bar-room philosophy. But we promise not to lecture you (well, not much), and we won't look embarrassed if you cry before closing time.

Afterwards, you ought to be buoyed up with confidence, safe in the knowledge that it really *isn't* just you. And so with any luck, when you are next downstairs at three in the morning and you know it should be time for the usual routine – screaming, wailing, rocking back and forth and demanding the comfort of the bottle – you'll be strong about it, and go and attend to the baby instead.

Chapter 2
The Kick Inside

Babies born in England and Wales in 2004: *621,469.*

 o it's come to that time – you have decided to make a baby. Understand that this means the following. You and your dearly beloved have, in effect, decided that:

- You'd like your house to look as if you have installed the chic 'Eastern European town after a particularly nasty civil war' look.
- You no longer want a social life. Apart, that is, from going to the sort of party where people scream loudly, sing 'The Wheels On The Bus' incessantly and trample Smartie-cakes into the carpet.
- You think sleep is overrated anyway.
- You have decided to give up your human rights and to begin acceding to the demands of a small, noisy terrorist.
- You're happy for most of your income to go to chemists, toy-shops and the Early Learning Centre.
- You've always thought you'd look quite distinguished with grey hair/no hair.

Welcome to the Pleasuredome
The best thing you can do is to learn from others. Make friends with a couple who are already parents, if you don't already know one. When you have done this:

✓ *Do* ask them questions. For instance, NCT (National Child-birth Trust) antenatal classes sometimes give you homework, some of which involves asking parents-you-know what the most useful and most useless item they own is. (See Chapter 23.)

✓ *Do* ensure that you coo over their little darlings, even when they are trying to shove drumsticks up your nose and smear your Louis Vuitton shirt with jam. When the time comes, you'll want people to be similarly admiring of yours.

✓ If they have literally just had the baby, cook them a hot meal and take it round. It's the one thing you find you just don't have time to do in the first few days – and you'll appreciate it when it's your turn.

✗ *Don't* upbraid the parent friends for their lack of discipline and patience.

✗ Try not to get the child's name wrong. You may not think there is much difference between Emma and Emily, or Joshua and James – but they will.

✗ *Don't* ask 'How do you find parenthood, then?' (Left at the first junction?)

✗ Refrain from tutting at the couple's low tolerance levels and hyperactive offspring.

✗ And I wouldn't suggest ways in which they might improve their children's sleeping habits, toilet training, table manners and overall behaviour. It will only end in tears. Yours, probably.

✗ *Don't* say 'I love kids but I couldn't eat a whole one.' It may be funny to you. They will have heard this a thousand times and will be heartily sick of it.

✗ You *don't* need to tell them when the baby is crying. Trust me, they will know almost without hearing it. So will you, soon enough.

Chapter 3
Possibly Maybe

The approximate world population in 2005 is *6 billion*.
The UN's forecast of the approximate world population
by 2050 is *10 billion*.

The 'are you emotionally ready?' quiz

1   You attended your niece/nephew's birthday party last year
    and you were the only man there without a child. How did
    that make you feel?
    a) Enormously relieved that you had a life to go back to.
    b) So bored that you were forced to make polite conversa-
       tion about holiday driving with a dull insurance sales-
       man.
    c) Slightly thoughtful and maudlin.

2   Going out and getting totally wrecked and crawling home
    at 3 a.m. is going to become something other people do, at
    least for a while. What's your reaction?
    a) You're kidding. How will I survive?
    b) I'll crack open the odd beer at home, I suppose. Not a big
       deal.
    c) Come on, getting drunk is juvenile anyway. I'm going to
       be responsible now.

3   Your oldest friend from school has a stag weekend/bach-
    elor party in Amsterdam planned for the date when your
    baby is due. What's your take on this?
    a) Livid – why the hell did it have to happen now?

b) A bit annoyed that you'll miss it, but never mind – this is more important.

c) What on earth's the point of a boozy weekend, anyway? Been there, done that.

4 You like your lie-in on a Sunday morning. How do you feel about this?

a) You intend to carry on having one, and no baby is going to stop you.

b) You're going to see if you can get away with it now and then.

c) Forget it.

5 For a holiday, the choice will be between (i) a windswept caravan site on the coast where you spend every day building sandcastles and flying kites, or (ii) a 'fun' holiday complex somewhere in Europe, surrounded by other families with screaming children. How do you react to this?

a) I'd rather have my toenails removed without anaesthetic.

b) Not my first choice, but if it makes them happy …

c) Great – just what I'd have chosen.

6 Your idea of a pleasant Saturday afternoon is:

a) Watching the football with your friends and then going on to the pub for a few pints.

b) Relaxing quietly at home with the family, reading the papers and maybe playing some games in the garden.

c) Running yourself ragged round a freezing cold playground and/or indoor play centre, while a small person attempts to escape from your sight and/or grasp, kicks you in the shins and spills the flask of tea you have brought along.

7 Your choice of drinking place is:
   a) A loud, packed city-centre bar where they show sport on a great big screen and play Basement Jaxx on the stereo, while lissom waitresses with pierced navels dance on the tables to bring you beer on trays.
   b) A friendly, buzzing country pub with a real log fire and a selection of home-cooked food.
   c) A soulless Fun Pub where you are allowed only one half of a middling beer and you get to eat a reheated steak and kidney pie with watery vegetables. Hundreds of screaming children throw food at one another while running to and from the 'Fun Area' with tomato-sauce-stained faces, you keep getting up to take yours to the toilet, and it's only a small comfort that everybody else looks as miserable as you do.

8 You're going to get a big night out some time between now and your next birthday, and so you imagine you're going to see:
   a) The hottest new band on the planet, playing at your local sweaty basement venue.
   b) *Puss In Boots*, featuring someone from *I'm A Celebrity, Get Me Out Of Here*.
   c) The *Noddy Roadshow*.

9 Children should:
   a) Be seen and not heard.
   b) Be tolerated.
   c) Be the centre of the universe.

10 Your entire life is about to become dictated by the whims, caprices and bodily fluids of a small dictator who cannot walk, talk, eat, sleep or defecate properly and is reliant on you for every single thing he/she needs doing. How does this make you feel?
    a) Terrified.
    b) Nervous.
    c) Fine.

If you scored …

- Mostly (a): This whole dad thing is going to take a bit more getting your head round. Keep reading.
- Mostly (b): You need a bit more brainwashing before you're ready, but basically you'll get by. Read on for a few more tips.
- Mostly (c): It seems you have girded your loins, battened down the hatches and are ready for fatherhood – well done. Are you sure you are actually human?

Chapter 4
Everybody's Changing

He came to me one day and said, 'I've never killed a tiger'.
I said, 'Why are you telling me?' 'Well, I've got to tell somebody!'
I thought all fathers were like this lunatic.
Spike Milligan (interviewed in *Q* Magazine in 1989)

Flexible preparation module: Part 1

ere are a few things you can do to practise the lifestyle of a parent. When you've seen your child through to the age of five, come back and read this again. You'll probably be able to add your own ideas.

a) Scribble all over your newest wallpaper, preferably in indelible marker-pen.
b) Find six new films that you'd quite like to see at the cinema. Don't see them. Say, 'It's okay, they'll all be on TV in a couple of years.' Ignore the friends who shake their heads in despair at this.
c) Buy six interesting-looking new books. Don't read them. Scribble on them. Rip the covers off them and shove them down the back of the sofa.
d) Buy six DVDs that you want to see. Don't watch them. Bend them into interesting shapes and smear them with yoghurt. Also put freshly buttered toast in the video.
e) Spend a long time making a meal following a complicated recipe. Make sure it is something which should, ideally, be eaten as soon as it's cooked. Then try eating it reheated, after two hours – or just put it in the bin and have fish and chips instead.

f) Same with cups of tea and coffee. Make them, take two or three sips and then leave them on the kitchen table to go cold. For added authenticity, get someone to spill a few on the carpet.

g) While you are on the phone to a friend, colleague or bank manager having a really important conversation, get someone to tug repeatedly on your trouser leg, saying either, 'Look at this, Daddy, look, look, look!' or, 'Me want to talk! Want to talk! It's not fair, *meeee* want to talk!'

h) Scenario to enact: you've been out for one too many and you're lying on the sofa with the father of all hangovers, thinking that you will just about be all right if it stays dark and quiet and you *lie really still*. Then get a small person to do the following: (i) barge in, (ii) fling a plastic fire-engine at you, (iii) switch on a *Postman Pat* video very loudly and (iv) thump you in the stomach, shouting, 'Play with me, Daddy, chase me, pick me up, now, *now*!!'

i) Make friends with someone who has a dog. Ideally it should be someone who is besotted with their pet. Then just listen. Their conversation is all about diet, worming, vaccination, tails, fleas, the vet, etc., etc. It will bemuse and bewilder you. This is *exactly* what it will be like for your non-parent friends after you have had your baby.

j) Get your other half to lie in bed kicking you at regular intervals. You can combine this with an alarm clock that goes off at midnight and every two hours thereafter.

k) Hold a 'conversation' (use the term loosely) with a very stoned friend – someone who is quite chatty and utterly charming, but also rather paranoid. They will demand that you follow every bizarre comment with an intelligent riposte, not just, 'Mmmm, oh yes.' They will get quite cross when you don't give exactly the expected response (without clues as to what that response should be). They will then eat all your crisps and chocolate. This is perfect training for a day with a toddler.

l)   And here's a big one – ask *everyone* you meet if they could, perhaps, give you some unsolicited tips on bringing up your children. Go for those who don't have children of their own in particular. They always have all the answers. We call them … *The Not-We*. You will encounter them again later in this book.

Flexible preparation module: Part 2

Also, if you use a computer at work or at home at all, there are a few key ways in which this will have prepared you for the task of having a child. Funnily enough, studies have shown that there are several key ways in which the child you produce will be *exactly like your computer*. For example:

- It will not respond to clear instructions.
- The manuals are incomprehensible and far too thick to read properly.
- It does all sorts of things you never suspected it could.
- A vast range of expensive accoutrements and add-ons is available, most of which you don't need.
- You worry unduly about how others might infect, corrupt and influence it.
- If you try to get it to do something it's not done before, it will decide it doesn't like this and will throw a hissy-fit.
- You get through enormous amounts of resources, most of which just end up in the bin.
- If you put rubbish in one end, rubbish will come out at the other end.
- You've had it five years and you still don't understand it properly.

- You're baffled by the messages it gives you.
- It sometimes makes strange noises which don't seem to mean anything.
- Too much time in its company will give you a headache.
- Some days, you are convinced it actually hates you.
- But when it does things right, you feel an enormous sense of relief, gratitude and love.

On the other hand, the same studies have isolated a number of ways in which *your computer is nothing like your child at all*. Here are the advantages of owning a PC, none of which apply, sadly, to your future offspring:

- It can be switched off when you want it to go to sleep.
- It doesn't actually answer back.
- You can deactivate its sound-chip.
- It will quite happily stay still in one place for years without being bored.
- No matter how much junk you feed into it, it won't get fat or ill.
- They are available in a wide range of colours and styles, and you can choose these beforehand.
- If it goes wrong, you don't need to feel guilty or inadequate if you have to call an expert in to fix it.
- You know there's nothing wrong with shielding it from the pernicious influence of the outside world.
- It doesn't need regular trips to playgrounds, ice-creams or other treats to keep it on your side.
- It doesn't scream.
- It doesn't smell (much).
- If you get sick of it, you can trade it in for a newer, better one.

Chapter 5
Treat Her Like a Lady

The UK fertility rate (average children per family unit) in 1971 was *2.4 children*.

on't forget your other half, your wife, your partner, your soulmate, the good lady, her indoors, the boss, the missus – or whichever of the many choices available you personally feel happiest with. You may have been with her since Kylie and Jason last appeared on *Top Of The Pops* together, or you may have just met at a speed-dating-and-curry evening down at the local church hall a few months ago. It doesn't matter. Now that she is carrying a small person around inside her, your relationship with her will change.

Here are some key moments in the nine months, with hints as to how you should behave in order to stay in her good books.

The discovery
She will probably come in, waving a white, pen-sized thing which looks a bit like some piece of gadgetry which Mr Spock would have used to determine the presence of alien life forms. (You're close.) The pregnancy test has come on in leaps and bounds in the last twenty years, and it's about as simple as it can get – basically, if there's a blue line in the box, then it's 'hello daddy'. As our doctor said at the time, 'They'll sometimes tell you that you're not pregnant when you really are, but they never tell you that you are when you're really not.' It's a good idea to look pleased and excited, even if the thought terrifies the life out of you. Give her a hug and a kiss and, while she is on the

phone telling her mum, her sister, her cousins, her hairdresser and 'everybody else who knows me' (as they say on the radio), return to your displacement activity. You'll have plenty of time to get used to the idea.

A lot of people choose not to tell the world at large until after the 12th week, because this is when the danger of an uncompleted pregnancy drops dramatically. Sadly, miscarriage is a fact of life and rather more common than you may believe; some studies say that 1 in 4 pregnancies will end in miscarriage, others put the figure as high as 1 in 3. Whatever the actual statistics, the chances are that you will know someone who's been through it – and there's a chance that it may happen to you.

Speaking from experience, the most upsetting thing is the sense of loss that you will both undeniably feel. If she is unfortunate enough to experience a miscarriage, this will be one of the most emotional and stressful times in your relationship, and a time when she will need you more than ever. Luckily, there is an excellent support network out there, spearheaded in the UK by the Miscarriage Association, and they come with a very warm recommendation: **www.miscarriageassociation.org.uk** is where they can be found. Outside the UK, **www.babyloss.com** features a selection of international support groups.

As time goes on

There are a number of things you can do in order to make life easier for you both while she is pregnant. Obviously you'll do a lot of the fetching and carrying, including getting her those odd mixtures of haddock and chocolate for which she will start to have cravings. And from about five months, get used to the little 'ooh' sound which she will make every time she gets up or sits down, accompanied by her placing her hand in the small of her back; this is usually the cue to either (a) fetch her a cushion or (b) say 'Can I do that for you, dear?'.

At about five months, the bump will start to show, and this is the point at which people start signing birthday cards 'from Percy, Demelza and Bump.' Others may even go down the zany route of purchasing an oversized 'Baby On Board' T-shirt. The wacky funsters.

This is the only time in your life when you may be able to remark how big she is looking and actually get away with it. It's still advisable, even now, to avoid that three-letter F-word, though; it can be a trigger for all sorts of unpleasantness. But you should avoid saying, 'Morning sickness? Can't you take anything for that?' (They tried – you may remember a few problems in the 1960s with a drug called thalidomide.) Oh, and while we're on a warning note, it's best not to say anything about her having 'retired' from work or being 'on holiday', either. That way lies the spare room.

The expectation of attendance

You are pretty much going to be there for the great occasion of your child's entry into the world. If, at the let's-make-a-baby stage, you were saying things like, 'I don't want to be there for the birth,' you may have found her countering it with, 'Well, don't expect to be there at the conception, then.'

If you have any friends who are already dads, you may find they will want to show off about how they got the day off work and were there for the birth – and so frankly if you're not, then you risk looking like a wimp. Anyway, if you've seen *Alien*, it should prepare you for what to expect.

You may argue that your dad wasn't there at your birth, nor your grandfather for your dad's. You may ask why your generation should be the one expected to take on all the baggage of birthing partnership and breathing exercises and knowing what a TENS machine is (I'll tell you later if you don't know) and all that sort of thing. You may have imagined yourself pacing a hospital corridor with your hair slightly tousled and your tie askew, having been summoned from work by the news that your wife was in the labour ward. You may envisage yourself being ushered into a nice clean room a few hours later to greet a scrubbed little pink baby wrapped in a towel. You may picture your tired but smiling beloved, a rosy-cheeked paragon of maternal pride in a hospital gown.

Sorry. It doesn't seem to happen that way any more. It's just the flipside of progress.

Anyway, cheer up. You may enjoy it.

Being prepared

A few days before the baby's due, you may like to have the *Emergency Labour Bag* somewhere prominent, like in the hall. For self-preservation it's sensible not to put it where someone could trip over it. (Someone like a fractious nine-months-pregnant woman who can no longer see her feet, just for instance.)

In the Emergency Labour Bag, you'll put everything she will need for the experience and for spending a couple of days in hospital: nightwear (pack three items for good measure), dressing gown and slippers, toiletries, large sanitary towels, breast-pads, a feeding bra (you'll have great fun buying this), some flannels and some towels. If you want to be really organized, you could even put in a few nappies. They'll have them in the hospital, but it's never too soon to start showing off your forethought.

Put a camera or camcorder in too – you may want to capture the moment. If it's not a digital, take some spare film. You'll find that even veterans of video nasties will be reluctant to watch actual 'during' footage, though – I'd wait until Baby has popped out before you start getting snap-happy or turning into Spielberg.

Also, pack *water* in the Emergency Labour Bag – nobody tells you this, but delivery rooms get very, very hot. She may tell you she doesn't want any, or even just want a sip or two. Let me explain: it's mainly for you. Oh, and bananas. These are good for slow energy release – labour can last a long time, you may need food, and you may not be in a position to pop down to the cafeteria.[1] And if you're planning to order beer and a pizza, it could be considered rude to rest it on the bump while you look at what's going on down there. A flask of ice cubes is useful too.

It will also be a good idea to have the midwife's telephone number written clearly somewhere near the phone. You'll need someone level-headed to talk to when you start to panic. But also, she'll need to know that you're on your way – either to hospital or to the plastic-lined room in your house which you have set aside for the occasion.

Another girl, another planet
Notes from all the antenatal consultations should go in the bag. You'll also have something called a *birth plan*, which you and she will have agreed with the midwife. (Well, she and the midwife will have agreed it, while you sat there, made tea and nodded a bit while trying to look as if you knew what they were talking about.) The birth plan is a document in which a mother specifies what pain relief she wants. These are the main options:

---

1   But if you are the well-organized type who will have this ready two or three weeks before the due date, it is advisable to change the bananas after a week.

- *TENS machine* (see, I said I'd tell you): A small electronic gizmo which tapes on to her back and is attached to a switch she can press. You can hire them from Boots. It stimulates endorphins and is supposed to reduce pain in the initial stages of labour. In the latter stages, we found, it's about as useful as a chocolate teapot.
- *Gas & Air*: The standard option, available to inhale from a face-mask. Bit of a misnomer, as it's actually an oxygen/nitrous oxide mix, and it will make her very thirsty. There is a theory that it's more the act of having something to do which provides relief, rather than the mixture itself. Don't have any yourself, however tempted you are.
- *Pethidine*: If you know enough chemistry, you may realize this is a synthetic version of morphine. I was told by my better half that it didn't do any good. Funnily enough, my suggestion that she would have been in even *more* pain without it was not graciously received. Bad Fact which may put you off: it's the substance which the notorious serial killer Dr Harold Shipman used on some of his victims.
- *Epidural*: Basically, an injection into the spine which numbs her totally. She won't feel anything at all, which can make it hard to push. You hear horror stories about them going wrong, which you're best off talking to your midwife about. It's probably scaremongering. Doctors like them, presumably as it makes their job easier (rather than making it easier on the mother), so that may be one good reason not to have one.

As a man, you may find the idea that some women want to give birth without pain relief, or just with some laughing gas and a bit of extra oxygen, a rather startling one. 'Women have done this for centuries,' so the wisdom goes, 'and they didn't need pethidine or epidurals back then. It's a natural process.'

Well, yes – but in those more innocent times, people also used to press leeches on to open wounds, treat pestilence with burning sulphur and amputate the odd limb with rusty farming implements. Now, I may be old-fashioned about this, but I do wonder if nostalgia, while all very well with fashion and music, is somewhat misplaced when it comes to pain-relief options. We don't live in the 21st century for nothing. Surely men would be much more pragmatic about the whole thing. You can't help thinking that, if it was you in there, you'd put your feet in the stirrups and say, 'Give me every drug you've got, sir – I want to be *in orbit* when it happens.'

In the birth plan, she also sets out all the delightful and restful things she would like to be happening while giving birth. In theory, this means that she wants to be having the baby while draped elegantly over a giant rubber ball and listening to whale song, or sprawled in a pool of jasmine-scented water eating truffles, or plumped up with cushions on her own bed of crisp white sheets and watching re-runs of *Heartbeat* on cable. She will set down in writing that she wishes to present the baby to the world in a natural environment, free of pain relief and medical intervention, perhaps glowing gently and smiling while she clasps your hand, the two of you united in your love and pleasure as the baby slips gently out. It's your role to make sure the birth plan is implemented and she gets exactly what she wants.

In practice, your role will be to duck as she clenches her fists, arches her back and screams, '*Give me the epidural, NOW!*'

Chapter 6
Do You Really Want to Hurt Me?

The UK fertility rate (average children per family unit) in 2001 was *1.6 children*.

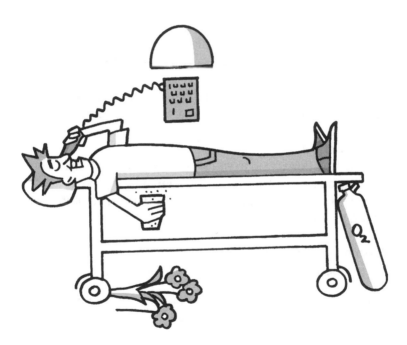

It's generally considered bad manners to ask a woman in labour to drive herself to the hospital (although it's not unheard of). The hospital may offer you transport, so do take advantage of this if you want; it all depends on how much you'd like to be rushed through the traffic in a screaming ambulance. Some people don't like to consider the act of childbirth to be a medical emergency and so would rather get there in more normal circumstances – or, indeed, would prefer to stay at home. It's something to be discussed in the months leading up to the birth. (As you'll know, you will usually have a good eight and a half of these at least, so there's no excuse for leaving the decision until your good lady is writhing on the sofa in contraction-induced agony.)

If you drive, you'll usually be all right to take her there yourself – the chances of junior emerging over the passenger seat really are minimal – although it's worth checking out the parking at the hospital beforehand.

If you get a taxi, it's up to you whether you ask the driver to go as fast as he can and risk bouncing everyone around, or take it gently and risk the excess fare for staining the seats with gore. Getting the bus is not advised.

When push comes to shove
During labour, only one rule really matters:

THERE IS NOTHING YOU CAN DO

If this were an email, I'd probably now do something like this :-)

You are there to provide 'emotional support'. But whatever you do, your beloved will probably be drugged up to the eyeballs and won't remember it afterwards anyway. She will still scream, swear and dig her fingernails deeply into your arm while pushing. Just be there – it is enough.

While doing nothing, you may like to bear some of the following points in mind. None of them will actually help, but they might make you feel a bit better.

- You can mop her fevered brow, as it looks useful.
- You can spend money on New Age accoutrements such as wind-chimes, whale song tapes, Enya CDs, *feng shui* and aromatherapy. It's up to you. It won't matter. You may as well play a pirate download of someone doing the Cult's 'Edie (Ciao Baby)' on the flugelhorn for all the difference it will make.
- Don't be alarmed if she suddenly seems to develop Tourette's. It's fair enough, really. Imagine that something the size of a melon was trying to push its way out from between your testicles – you'd say something a little stronger than, 'Gosh, that stings a bit.' Just remember, to paraphrase the words sung by Bono in 'Do They Know It's Christmas', that 'Tonight, thank God it's her, instead of you.'
- Listen to what the midwife says – she'll probably give you a running commentary on the baby's progress, in the manner of a commentator describing a really exciting horse race. ('And coming up now on the near side, it's New Baby, New Baby is almost there, we're into the final furlong and New Baby is going to take it …' OK, not quite like that, but you get the idea.)
- You'll probably have to relay all this to your dearest, as she will be too busy pushing as if … well, as if going to the toilet for the first time in a week. There are similarities, apparently.

As you'll have gathered by this point, it will not, repeat *not*, be like any birth you have ever seen in a popular TV drama. It will especially not be like that episode of *Neighbours* in 1989 in which Daphne, defying the laws of physics, gave birth without even taking her dungarees off.

Assuming it's a natural birth, at some point a baby will be the result of all this pushing. You may be given the chance to cut the umbilical cord. Depending on how you feel about such things, this may make you come over all masculine and primal and important, and you'll want to grasp the scissors firmly with both hands, doing a firm snip and pretending for a second that you are George Clooney in *ER*. On the other hand, you may demur, deciding that anything involving sharp implements and flesh is best left to those who do this sort of thing every day. Up to you.

Don't be alarmed if the little newcomer appears to be extremely slippery, gunky and red. Remember where he's just been, after all. (Again, it won't look anything like the ones on TV, which are usually clean and chubby three-month-olds.) The midwife will usually give Baby a wipe down before wrapping him in a towel and letting you have a hold. He's yours. Don't quake too much.

Oh, and shortly after the birth, something which resembles a giant plate of throbbing red and grey gristle will slither from your wife's nether regions. This is not the point to blanch and say, 'I didn't know there was another one up there. What an ugly specimen.' This is the placenta, and you don't need it. You can usually do what you like with it. Some people plant it in the garden to fertilize the soil. Others have it packed up and take it home to fry up with a nice bit of bacon (or tofu) and onions. Others are quite happy to let the professionals dispose of it in ways it's best not to know about, thanks.

Despite all this, do try not to faint. It's bad form. Of the three people needing to be looked after in the room, you'll be third on the list.

She'll need a bit of time to recover. Don't look down there for a couple of days if you are squeamish.

And furthermore:

✗ Never …

Ask her 'Did it really hurt that much?'

✓ Always …

Congratulate her immediately afterwards and tell her how clever she is for giving birth to such a lovely baby. It's probably best not to mention that she needs a bath.

Time to go home

A lot will depend on the time of day when the baby is born and what your hospital's policy is, but you can't always stay overnight with mother and baby. (You get to go home and nurse your headache with paracetamol and coffee, or maybe something a bit stronger. Lucky you. It won't all quite have sunk in yet, so make the most of your last night without a small person in the house.) Hospitals used to encourage mothers to stay in for a while – there are things they need to learn, after all. Believe it or not, women weren't born knowing how to breastfeed, and they need a bit of practice to get it right. These days, with the bed shortages the way they are, nursing mothers are pretty much turned out on to the street as soon as is decent. Sometimes before.

You also get to do another of the fun bits, which is phoning up *The List Of People* to tell them of the new arrival. You may already have called the immediate relatives from the hospital, but you'll have a longer list to work your way down once you get home. If the baby was born in the early hours of the morning and you get home just as dawn is breaking, it can be quite fun to dose yourself up with coffee, settle down in an armchair and give some of your more hard-partying, night-owlish friends an unexpected morning call. When they find out what it's for, there's no way they'll be able to be cross with you.

Some time after your child is born, you will find yourself on the phone to your friends again. 'Oh, yes,' you'll be saying, 'three weeks since the birth. Yes, she can wiggle her toes a bit, smile, sort of gurgle … and Baby's not doing badly either.'

Chapter 7
World Shut Your Mouth

An inevitable truth: People will be lining up to give you well-intentioned advice.

t seems that, as soon as you become a parent, normal social niceties are suspended and people think they can criticize whatever they like. Everyone from best friends to complete strangers will be leaning into the pram and passing comment: on the ill-matched clothes, the gurgling apology for speech, the strands of wispy hair, the weird eating and drinking habits and the fragmented sleep routine. And when they've finished laying into you, they'll move on to the baby.

Quite often, the people giving the advice will not have had to deal with a small child for several years, even decades – or possibly ever. In some places, I believe this is known as 'unmarried marriage-counsellor syndrome'. And as for the professionals … well, let's come to them in a minute.

You, on the other hand, are learning on the job, and you will have a pretty rapid learning curve too. Trust your own instincts – and don't compare yourself with other dads, for that way lies eternal frustration.

Enlightenment

The vast majority of parents will feel helpless at some point, and some of them will actually go and seek out help.

The problem is, there are so many parenting manuals on the market, full of desperately po-faced if well-intentioned advice. You'll also suddenly start seeing whole new sections of the magazine stands which you had previously just ignored. And I don't just mean the thinly-written, headache-inducing catalogues which pass for children's comics these days. Move along. Go past the car magazines and the sci-fi and the stamp-collecting and look there. Yes, *there* – next to all the women's stuff. Now there's a coincidence. Or not.

Yes, I mean *the parenting magazines*. Just stand and look at them for five minutes. Observe, in passing, how nearly all of them feature well-groomed mothers with beautiful children on the cover, and how few, if any, have a dad pictured anywhere in sight – no, not even up to his arms in cot-building or similar manly activity somewhere in the background. Well, people think they want them – one look at these magazines' circulations should confirm that. They have, of course, one big advantage over the likes of *Stamp Collecting Weekly* and *Fisherman's Companion*, namely an endlessly self-renewing readership. People might stop reading them as their children get older, but there will always be new readers lining up to take their place. In 2004, the number of babies born in England and Wales rose by 4% to 621,469 – the highest birth rate for five years and the biggest rise for 25 years. (Those schools are going to get pretty crowded. See Chapter 37 for more on that.) And so all those new parents are out there, needing help, reaching for it in a competitively priced package ... a captive audience.

Then there are *the newspaper articles*. If you get a paper every week, then pretty soon you'll find *that* article. You know – the one by the mother who wants to share her starry-eyed 'I'm the first woman ever to have a baby and isn't it awful/wonderful/perplexing' platitudes with the rest of the world. The same article will be rehashed every three months or so, each time by a different journalist but each time with the same breathy zeal. You've probably seen the kind of thing: 'Well! Eight months to go and I've been throwing up every morning ...' Also in the parenting pages, you can read about the latest feeding bottles, designer buggies and techniques in baby massage. Occasionally you'll read cheerful, jokey pieces in which baby Pilates and baby yoga are given a test run by four women, usually a quartet of Hampstead mums who were at college with the journalist.

Others report (gleefully?) on the stratospheric costs of raising a child.

But still more of them, these days, focus on the many and varied things you are probably doing which make you a bad parent. That's everything from feeding your child non-organic milk to sending him to a day nursery. You mean to say you buy Heinz baby jars rather than boiling and mashing your own organic butternut squash? What, you let her watch half an hour of *The Magic Roundabout* at bedtime rather than doing holistic crystal therapy exercises together? Call yourself a dad? How do you dare show your face in public? You start to feel like those actors and writers who never open a newspaper because they fear reading a scathing review of their work.

Bad dad

Once you have been thoroughly lambasted and made to feel like a pathetic apology for a father, there are books and courses out there ready to break you down still further and rebuild you in their image. Supernannies, child psychologists, parent coaches, child managers with their five-step plans presented on Power-Point … You do sometimes wonder how our own parents got by without them. And if only our grandparents, cowering with their families in air-raid shelters, had been given an integrated programme of stress counselling and gestalt therapy. How did previous generations manage without *feng shui* consultants, crystal healing and life coaches? What an impoverished world they all must have lived in.

And then, of course, we have the plethora of TV programmes which blame you for everything. In the 1990s we had endless househunting and home-improvement shows clogging up the schedules, but now the latest car-crash TV fad is mum-and-dad-bashing. Yes, it's true – parenting is the new interior design.

Your baby isn't eating, defecating and sleeping to order? Right, that's your fault! Your child won't ever do as she's told? Well, there must be something wrong with you as a parent! Get with the programme and get in the Boot Camp For Tiny Terrors!

Of course, your children's behaviour is your responsibility and you shouldn't try to foist the blame on anybody else when they turn into little vandals and hooligans. And nor can you start moaning about the school's sex education policy if your daughter turns into a 13-year-old mum with a baby called Jay-Zee Versace, or blame society if your sweet toddler becomes a thug with an electronic tag.

But here's a revelation: you aren't automatically a bad parent if you don't enjoy being with your baby or toddler 24 hours a day. It doesn't mean you don't love them. All relationships have their ups and downs. Sometimes, they will drive you mad. Sometimes, work will feel like a blessed escape. And sometimes, you will be counting the minutes until story time. Singing their songs and playing their repetitive games is not something which you *must* feel endless ecstasy about. It doesn't mean you're not making them feel loved, and wanted, and safe.

It's unlikely that this frustration is an invention of the 21st century. But for the first time, we have an entire industry devoted to making us feeling guilty about it. We are hardly the first generation of stressed-out, anxious and paranoid parents. On the other hand, we are the first generation of stressed-out, anxious and paranoid parents who think that we'll solve everything by throwing money at a consultant.

I wonder if you have ever been sent on a course for work and, halfway through a mind-numbing day, have thought to yourself in frustration and anger, 'I could have put this presentation together myself. It's hardly rocket science.' The same often goes for the advice given about children. So I need to spend more time playing with my kids? You don't say! We need to try to shout at them a bit less and reason with them a bit more? I'd never have thought of that! I need to create some time once a week where my wife and I can have some time together without the kids around? Well, that would never have occurred to me! All this time, people have been queuing up to take the children off my hands so that we could go out for an Italian meal and a trip to the theatre, and I was selfishly turning them down just so that we could have an extra game of 'Disney Princess Snap' or another round of 'Who Hates Vegetables Tonight?' I don't know what I'd do without you, child experts. I fall at your feet.

Yes, more often than not, your greatest enemy is not frustration, tiredness, anger or the song repertoire of the Tweenies. It is what Basil Fawlty once referred to as 'Specialist Subject: The Bleedin' Obvious'.

Chapter 8
Boulevard
of Broken Dreams

*'How sharper than a serpent's tooth it is
To have a thankless child!'*
Shakespeare, *King Lear*, Act I Scene 4.

hat they don't tell you in antenatal classes, and what they rarely tell you in serious parenting manuals, is that your average baby or toddler is, basically, a terrorist.

They say the first thirteen weeks are the worst. Well, I say *they*. Who are they? Some of the parents I spoke to before having a child, that's who. And, in truth, only some of them say this. Some say it's the first thirteen months. Others say the first thirteen years are terrible, but from then on you know where you are as it's just hellish until they are twenty-one. Trust no one, I'd say.

Survival
For now your life gets put on hold for a bit. Here are a few of the things you can't do now you have a baby:

- Go to the pub.
- Go to the cinema.
- Go to the theatre.
- Read a book.
- Go to football/cricket/rugby matches.
- Have impromptu sex on the living-room floor.
- Have any sort of sex, anywhere.
- Have a lie-in.
- Enjoy staying up late.
- Play lots of PlayStation games.
- Talk at normal volume.
- Have conversations with non-parent friends.
- Have conversations which don't involve children.
- Have conversations.
- Go on an adventure holiday.
- Have a life.

Join our club

Your other half's main source of entertainment at this time will be ringing up all her friends and describing the birth process to them in intimate, excruciating detail. You have to wonder why she does this, but it makes her happy. She – and you – would do well to remember some trenchant advice: 'Not everything is an anecdote.' Some people will just not be 100% fascinated by the exact progression of her dilation, the amount of blood expended and the state of her nether regions afterwards. You may well be the second most interested, at around 80% (but much of that will be duty and/or horrified fascination), closely followed by pregnant friends at about 75%. Female friends who are 'trying' will possibly be next, at around 50–60%, followed by those in relationships who may want children at some point (35–40%). And frankly, singletons and the 'child-free' will want to hear it about as much as they'd want to hear the story of somebody's colonic irrigation.

In a few months it will be very different. Your soulmate will have forgotten just how painful the whole thing was and will be looking longingly at couples who have one toddler and one baby. That'll be time for a serious conversation. Get beer in.

Time of your life

When you first get your baby home, you have to do *everything* for him. This will probably make you absolutely terrified, which is perfectly normal. You have a small, helpless creature lying there who is incapable of doing anything for himself, and you are now in charge. This is probably where you'll find yourself most reliant on all those parenting manuals and baby books, monitoring every little gurgle and snort and trying to interpret what it all means, from the colour of the poo to the patterns of sleep. No point trying to tell you not to worry, because you will. Everyone does.

And if you really miss your social life, then remind yourself that Staying In is the new Going Out. Obviously it's not really.

That would be silly. It's one of those ideas that magazine features editors throw on the table when they are really desperate:

'Okay, Jemima, darling, we've had to drop the three-page spread on Celebrity Colonic Irrigation, it's just not very *now*. What can we do instead?'

'Got the very thing, Cressie. I'm thinking Staying In is the new Going Out.'

'Didn't we do that a couple of years back? And wasn't it just a crappy feel-good piece for people with no social life?'

'Yes, but then it flipped back and Going Out was the new Staying In. This'll be revolutionary. It's early-century retro-chic, like *Big Brother* nostalgia and Britney Spears doing a *Greatest Hits*.'

'Sounds cooool. What's the angle?'

'It's, like, very *now*? Takeaways, snuggling on the sofa, Saturday night TV on the upswing? Should go down a storm with young parents.'

'Brilliant. So is that really the angle?'

'Well, no. Basically it's a crappy feel-good piece for people with no social life again.'

'Super. What's next?'

'Maximalism is the new Minimalism?'

'Cool.'

So yes, you'll have to adjust your life, but there are a few things you can do to remind yourself that it's not all bad. Gazing thoughtfully and lovingly at your child while she is asleep is sometimes recommended, as it is the time when they look their most beautiful and peaceful (although you may be so desperate for sleep yourself that you'll decide not to bother).

Remember, it's not just you.

Chapter 9

Don't Call Me Baby

- *20%* of parents chose the child's name after he/she was born.
- *11%* did so 'when' he/she was born. (Presumably this means at some point during the mess and grunting and before the 'Congratulations!')
- *67%* – an amazingly high proportion, if you ask me – made the choice before the child was born. It must have come as quite a shock to Mr and Mrs Jones's little boy that they'd already decided to call him Britney.[1]

You may have decided well in advance what to call your child, or you may not have a clue. A survey by *Junior* magazine in 2004 revealed the statistics above. Whatever the case, you'll need something up your sleeve for when you go and register the birth. The hospital will usually give you some documentation to take along, and you'll need to ring up for an appointment and go along at the appointed time.

If you're married, it's a straightforward Dad's Job. Your other half will still be making little 'ooh' noises whenever she gets up or sits down (fair enough, really, given the major bomb-in-an-offal-factory incident that's just happened down there) and will also probably have a small person gnawing away at each of her breasts in turn. So enjoy it – it's painless, gets you out of the house for a bit and feels all official and grown-up.

---

1 And if you're good at maths and are adding up right now – no, it's not recorded what option the other 2% went for. Maybe they decided to be radical and not give Baby a name at all.

If you're not married, it's a bit more complicated and there are various ways of getting the father's name on to the birth certificate – basically, it boils down to one of you signing a declaration or the two of you going along together. Ask your local council about this.

The registrar enters your details on a computer. Make sure you know where you and your other half were both born and have a handy description of your job(s). This may sound obvious, but it isn't always easy. They also inscribe the details in a rather grand-looking ledger with an old-fashioned fountain pen, which makes it all feel rather splendid.

By any other name
If you are having trouble coming up with names, bear the following in mind.

✓ At least talk about names before the birth, because you'll have a lot of other things to consider once it's all happened – and you don't want to feel rushed into making a decision. There's only so long that the midwife can keep referring to 'Baby' when she comes to visit. Think how you'd like it if you were only known as 'Big Person'.
✓ *Do* check out the name books. There are more than enough on the market, some of which will give you derivations going back centuries – or at least as far as 2002, assuming you should wish to inflict the name Chardonnay on your daughter. Don't laugh. More than 40 parents, presumably big fans of the TV series *Footballers' Wives*, have already done so.
✓ *Do* think carefully about where they may be growing up and going to school; the poor child will have to live with the name for life. All those parents who named their daughter Gaye after the hit Clifford T. Ward song in 1973 must, at some point,

have had a little twinge of regret. And the name Gabriel is a noble one and may yet enjoy a renaissance, but it would be a lucky boy indeed who didn't get mercilessly teased with the obvious nickname at school.

✓ Be circumspect, but not paranoid. A parenting forum on the Internet recently devoted a lot of space to a mum's groundless fear that calling her son the fine name of William would result in his cruelly being nicknamed Willy. One can also dismiss similar fears about Richard/Dick – although maybe think twice if your surname is Head, Braine or Small. But think carefully, saying the name aloud with the surname too. There is at least one Euan Kerr out there. (Yes, really. He's editor of *The Dandy*, and so I'm sure he is man enough to have taken the jokes on the chin.)

✓ Think about the initials too. It may sound lovely to call your child (for instance) Nicholas Oliver Bernard or Andrew Richard Simon, but that won't spare his blushes when he comes to initial a document in later life.

✓ And I suppose if your surname is one of those which, through no fault of your own, people find amusing – say, Smellie or Lillicrap or Slapper – then the best you can do for your child is to deflect it with a dull first name.

✓ *Do* resist family pressure, if there is any, to use great-grandparents' names and others which have been in the family for decades, unless you personally want to. Previous generations' names go in and out of fashion without any apparent logic: Emily, Jack, Oscar and Molly are all enjoying a splendid revival, but Walter, Maud, Agnes and Ernest have yet to see theirs. Good, solid names from the 1960s – John, Susan, Peter, Stephen, Sarah – have now dropped off the chart altogether and are no doubt awaiting their own renaissance in decades to come. The biggest new entry in recent years is Mohammed. (If you're not a Moslem, it's a brave choice.)

✗ *Don't* choose something with a daft spelling. The school registers of the 1990s were blighted by mums' addiction to *Ricki Lake* during maternity leave. Well, there must be *some* explanation for all those Tiffanees, Lateeshas, Kristoffers, Jaysens and Mikkaelas. (Okay, so I am lobbing rocks from the limited cover of my greenhouse here, given the number of times I've had to point out that my daughter's name is spelt 'the Jane Austen way'.)

✗ It used to be a common custom for the first-born son to be named after his dad. This doesn't happen so often now, and with good reason: you don't want to be known for ever as Big Dave and Little Dave. And anyway, imagine the potential for embarrassing mix-ups on the phone. 'Oh, hello, is that Dave Blenkinsop? ... Hi, Dave, it's the clinic here. We've got your results ...'

✗ Please, please, *don't* inflict every name from your favourite sports team on your son. It may seem pretty cool for about two years, but it will rapidly become embarrassing when (a) it dawns on you that Number One Son is lumbered with the names of 11 footballers who could only scrape a 2–2 draw with the international giants of Macedonia, and (b) you realize the boy has 11 or even 15 first names – and that this, however you spin it, will make him look stupid.

✗ And yes – similar reservations also apply to naming him after all six James Bonds, all ten members of *Blake's 7* or even all the Apostles. (I knew a bloke called Judas once – can't imagine what thought process his parents went through.)

✗ But after all that, *don't* worry. Your child can always change his/her name by deed poll in later life if they really, really hate it. Remember, a baby by any other name will still smell of wee.

Chapter 10
Nothing Can Stop Us

'A week is a long time in politics.'
Attributed to Harold Wilson.

What we learned in our first week

1 New babies are really light. It's like picking up a pack of prawn crackers. However, you don't realize this at the time – they seem heavy for the small size they are. You'll only actually notice it when, after a year or so of hefting your own infant, you have a hold of someone else's new baby, expecting to brace your legs like a weightlifter and get ready to put your back out as usual, and you're astonished by how little effort you need to lift him.

2 A baby always seems to be hungry. As long as she's awake, you cannot seem to overfeed her. Think of a petrol tank; it's not full unless it starts dribbling out of the top. They seem to know when they've had enough, and will certainly tell you (in their own inimitable way) when they haven't.

3 Six hours' sleep is an astonishing luxury which you will come to cherish. You can't quite understand how, in your younger days, staying up all night was seen as a really cool and zany thing to do. You start wishing that you had stored up your sleep when you were younger, or maybe kept some in a high-interest sleep account.

4 If someone says 'my baby's really good, he/she sleeps right through', understand that what they actually *mean* is that he/she only wakes up for feeds – e.g. at two, four and six in the morning – rather than bawling through the night.

They don't mean they are actually getting an uninterrupted night's sleep. That would be silly.

5   Nappy changing is, on balance, nowhere near as bad as people make out. It's all about damage limitation – see Chapter 11 for more details …

6   When wiping Baby's bottom, cotton-wool balls are better than pleats. This is because you only need one hand for them. This might seem like a really minor, trivial thing, but it could make the difference between your baby rolling off the table and not doing so.

7   You can never have too many nappies. Keep buying them. You will have to get used to it: you have about three years of piling them into the supermarket trolley ahead of you.

8   You can never have too many sleepsuits and vests. Keep washing them. It will amaze you how quickly they become too tight on your infant. Babies tend to lose a bit of weight after the birth, but then they pile it on. The weigh-in at the midwife's visit is a real eye-opener.

9   You will never forget the first time you hold your baby.

10   After one week, you will be so smug about what you've learned that you will be keen to pass on your knowledge to any prospective parents you happen to know. Probably with a strange, manic glint in your eye.

Chapter 11

One Cool Remove

Another inevitable truth: Babies are very, very messy.

The good dad's guide to poo

Y ou may think the word 'poo' is revoltingly infantile. It is, but get used to it. You have an infant, who is often revolting. 'Faeces' is a term you will only find in medical notes and your old fifth-form biology textbook, while 'crap' is not usually heard in front of children until they've had at least a couple of weeks in Reception class.

There are essentially only three main types of poo – vile, disgusting and stomach-churning. There is only one type of successful nappy-change – the one where you get it on Baby properly. This isn't the Olympics. Nobody is scoring you for technique. If you have enough antiseptic wipes and a strong enough stomach, it really doesn't matter what hair-curling horrors you have to encounter. *Just get it done*.

What comes out of a baby's bottom will at first be almost liquid, and might unexpectedly catch you on the hop – necessitating an early change of shirt for you, or even a re-decoration of the nursery. You'll become adept at having the new nappy standing up like the Thames Barrier in miniature, while you swab the infant down and bag up the soiled nappy.

Also, get used to sniffing Baby's bottom in public to see if he's done anything. This may sound like a horrific task, but it's not that bad once you become adept at it – and it's infinitely preferable to the alternative, which is sticking a finger inside the seam of the nappy and seeing if it comes out clean. I told you so.

The Nappy Conversation: the essentials in a nutshell.

'Use disposables. Seriously.'

'Oh, come on. What about all those landfill sites packed with festering nappies?'

'I know it doesn't make me an ethically sound, PC person, but this is the twenty-first century. Nobody says we ought to write with quill pens any more because of their beautiful aesthetics, or wear hessian because it's so versatile.'

'I dunno. What about the environment? You do realize we're going to run out of space for all this rubbish?'

'Look, if my conscience smarts, I'll give money to charity, do an old lady's shopping, recycle my aluminium. Or something. Anything. Have you read *Superwoman* by Shirley Conran? She says life's too short to stuff a mushroom. Well, Superdad – life's too short to wash a nappy.'

'Hmmm. Our parents did it, though. It doesn't take much – you just have to scape off the horrible stuff, then chuck it in that bucket with the detergent to soak. It doesn't exactly take much extra time. You just have to be a bit more organized.'

'Stop, stop! Enough already! I don't do *scraping*. Nappies don't just get a bit grubby. They don't just have little stains on them like ordinary people's clothes. A filthy nappy is a *vile* object. Your mission's to remove the thing, bag it up, bin it, wipe darling one's bottom clean and replace the offensive object with a fresh one. On a good day, you can do this in under a minute.'

'You're not convinced you're helping to cause an environmental disaster, then? Surely we should all be doing our bit. If everyone was like you, the world would be heading for meltdown.'

'Look, I'm sure you're right. But at the end of the day (or should I say, the end of the world), our little ball of dust is going to evaporate anyway when our sun burns through to its own core, and that's if we don't all manage to blow ourselves up first.'

'You're such an optimist.'

'Okay, what about the resources you use up with washables? The oceans of detergent, the small nuclear power station you'll need for powering all that washing and drying?'

'Depends if you do it efficiently. How about this – you do know disposables cost a fortune? Think how many thousands of nappies you're going to get through in, say, three years. You could be spending that money elsewhere.'

'Shop's own brand is good enough. It's not like it has to be a luxury item, for goodness' sake.'

'And I suppose you're going to get one of those, whassit, Sangenic things that packs them up in sausage-shaped parcels? Where they hang around the house for days?'

'Nah, just bung it in a bag. Look, they use the word "fragranced" in the adverts, and if you ask me that just seems *wrong* when you're not talking about air-freshener or washing-up liquid.'

As they say on *Big Brother*: 'You decide.'

Ch-ch-ch-changes (turn and face the strain)

Things are much better now than they were a decade ago, when you might have found a baby changing room in a shop or pub if you were lucky, but you couldn't count on it. And it would have been a 'Mother and Baby' room as well – it was no place for dads.

These days, such facilities are more the norm. Often, you'll find, they double up as the disabled toilet. They sometimes come equipped with a fold-down changing table, although getting this down is sometimes like putting up a deckchair – don't forget you'll be holding a writhing infant at the same time. If an establishment advertises itself as 'child-friendly' and doesn't have suitable changing facilities – or, indeed, falls short of catering for smaller customers in any other way – please send me an email to 'name and shame' them (**dan80s@hotmail.com**) and we'll try and build up a list. See Chapter 13 for a bit more on eating out with children.

Some institutions, though, do make an effort to cater for their small customers' ablutions. As I'm happy to 'name and praise' too, we've noticed Girl and Boy toilets in addition to Gents and Ladies in some *Brewer's Fayre* pubs, plus washbasins and hand dryers at a child-friendly height in *Pizza Hut*. Simple ideas, and they make all the difference.

But please, if you change your baby either on a park bench, or in the crowded carriage of a train, or on a pub table, remember that there are Not-We around, and they might not have such an effective in-built stench filter as you. Try to imagine how you would have felt if it had happened to you in your Non-Parent Days.

We effected a few pretty deft nappy changes on the front seat of a small car in our time – occasioned by necessity, not choice. On the whole this worked surprisingly well, I'd say. You're usually best advised to place one person on swabbing duty and stand the other guard in front of the car window. Your baby's bits may not be offensive to you, but there may be more delicate souls passing by.

Sometimes, even all the necessary precautions just won't prevent accidents. Darling Daughter did once manage a quite spectacular soiling which defied all standard attempts to combat it. It was the end of her first birthday, when we were driving back to Sheffield from her grandparents' house in Nottingham, a journey of about an hour. She'd had an exciting day, with lots of cake and running around and being the centre of attention. As we approached our fair city, it became apparent that she had managed to pass a liquid bowel movement right through the nappy, through two layers of clothing, through the padded car seat and on to the passenger seat below, where it collected like molten lava in a caldora. I don't think it's any coincidence that she was, at the time, listening on the radio to the UK entry in the Eurovision Song Contest, which that year managed to come 16th. (I won't embarrass the entrant. You can look it up.)

Anyway, after a good hose down and a sluice with disinfectant, I'm pleased to say the car furnishings were back to normal – or what passes for normal in a second-hand Vauxhall Astra. We managed to sell the car a couple of years later, and nobody commented on the strange stain.

Everything will flow

It isn't just the rear end that you need to worry about. Small babies – and not-so-small babies and toddlers, for that matter – seem to be engaged in a continual competition with one another as to who can produce the most liquids from the available orifices in any 24-hour period. It's as if there is some sort of reality game show happening on Baby TV that we don't know about. 'Right, William, that's two snot-bursts, gives you two points, so that puts you just three behind Tabitha, as she's just been sick down her mum's back! Ooh, no, hang on – Cameron's just had an Incredible Exploding Bottom five minutes before a christening, so that gives him ten points and that puts him clearly in the lead! Vote now for who *you* want to evict from the Cot for having the most disgusting nappy …'

The truth about vomit

Some babies are sick a lot, others aren't. You may be lucky, you may not. Usually, it's more of a dribble than a full-on projectile – unless they are sickening for something, in which case think *The Exorcist*.

Chapter 12
She Drives Me Crazy

transportation *n.* **1.** the act of conveying or the process of being conveyed.
2. removal to a penal colony.

There are distinct advantages to having a spring or summer baby, the biggest of which is that you can take them outside without having to wrap them up in sixteen layers of industrial insulation. Going for a walk with your child for the first time is a proud moment; be prepared to be stopped by doting old ladies, broody couples and, if you are alone with Baby, a few attractive young women.[1]

There are various ways of getting your baby around before he can walk, and they all have their good and bad points.

Carrying in your arms

Not to be dismissed lightly – you'll find yourself doing this a lot more than you may imagine. Sometimes it's just the easiest way to get Baby from A to B without having to go through the rigmarole of strapping him into something.

As he gets older, of course, and can walk, he will object to the idea of going from A to B without first passing through X, picking up Y and knocking Z to pieces. Any attempts to convey him like a babe in arms will inevitably be countered by a wave of toddler fury: screaming, wailing, wriggling and sometimes even biting. Between about 18 months and two, some toddlers perfect the 'Ironing Board' manoeuvre, where they lift their arms straight above their heads and straighten their legs, thus making themselves flat as a board and impossible to hold on to. All of them seem to know how to do this; it's as if they have learnt it at some secret training college.

---

1   If you mention the last bit to any single brothers or friends, they may then want to borrow Baby as an accessory. How you handle this is up to you. It could be the move that gives you a valuable hour or two's respite – if you trust them …

Wheelbarrow
Hours of fun in the garden, but has limited application for actually transporting her anywhere more interesting. Still, it will probably be her only experience of one-wheeled travel, unless she develops a career as a unicyclist.

Shopping trolley
Convenient even after she can walk, as it stops her from wandering off and getting lost in Household Goods. They usually love it – they sit there looking wide-eyed and contented. They think they're getting a free ride, while you know they are actually imprisoned. Everybody wins.

Slings
Yes, you too can be New Man, striding around with your offspring attached to your front as if in imitation of a pregnant woman. You can see the little head poking up and trying to peer over your shoulder, which is great fun. This method of transport means you can go for country walks on bumpy terrain, should you wish to do so – something which a pushchair's suspension finds it hard to cope with. Unfortunately, slings are not the easiest objects to get a baby into, and you'll always have that nagging feeling that he is about to drop out.

Backpacks
Here's another option, and it's one which enables you to experience once again what it's like to be an Inter-Railer. You get the same suspicious looks on public transport and the same people tutting as they have to duck when you swing around. It's all the more fun when you think that your burden isn't composed of guidebooks and clothes and souvenirs, but rather a sniffly, unsettled small person who is liable to vomit down the

back of the nearest stranger. It adds a frisson of risk, if you're into that kind of thing.

Pushchairs and prams

Nobody really has a *pram* any more, at least not in the sense that your grandma would have understood the word, i.e. a great, trundling thing made of reinforced industrial cloth, with spoked wheels and an armoured handle. If you do see anybody with one, the chances are that it's some sort of family heirloom and/or is being used for purely superstitious reasons.

The baby travel-unit seems to have morphed into the standard and ubiquitous *buggy*, which is fine until you have a warmongering toddler hanging off the buggy board. Buggies never have handles high enough, either, so you'll develop a stoop. If you have long legs, you always feel that you're doing something out of John Cleese's 'Ministry Of Silly Walks' in order to keep at the right level.

There's also the chunky *three-wheeler*, which is a bit silly if you live in a town or city; it makes it look as if your child is ensconced in its own personal armoured attack vehicle. This suits the siege mentality of the average baby, whose role model is Stewie from the cartoon *Family Guy* and who would probably quite like to have a cool gun turret and caterpillar tracks as well.

It's odd, but as soon as you have a pushchair of your own, your whole attitude to them changes somewhat.

In your previous life as a Not-We, you will perhaps have tried to do your shopping at the local out-of-town shopping complex at the weekend and will have tutted endlessly at the selfishness of the mothers charging you down in their reinforced three-wheelers. You'll have wondered why they should expect everyone else to get out of *their* way, and why they can't do their shopping during the week when everyone else is at work. You may, in a moment of heady rage, have even considered writing a letter to the local council requesting 'pushchair-free' days (to go along with the pensioner-free and student-free days you have already been demanding).

Now that you own a small baby tank, though, you'll start to realize just why you should be accorded space and a free path to the nearest exit. For a start, a buggy isn't that easy to manoeuvre – it's slightly more manageable than a shopping trolley, but not much. Secondly, you'll come to realize that, sometimes, speed is of the essence – for example, when a change or a feed is on the cards, and the parent and baby rooms are conveniently located three floors up. And you know what? Those selfish Not-We just *won't get out of your way*.

Pushchairs supposedly have brakes, but they are usually laughable devices – just a simple mechanical lever designed to immobilize the wheels. These usually work perfectly well for about the first thirty seconds of any journey on public transport. After that, your buggy will start to roll and bump around the aisle – to the delighted squeals of your infant, and to the agonized screams of the fellow passenger you have just kneecapped.

You can usually pile shopping under the buggy, but be warned – it's a great place for babies and toddlers to hide the booty which they inadvertently steal as you are walking round. It's not unusual to come back from Sainsbury's and wonder why on earth you have bought three parsnips, a tube of denture fixative and a Tony Christie album. The small, moon-faced kleptomaniac sitting in front of you will feign innocence; believe none of it. It's between you and your conscience whether you actually return any of this stuff.

Bear in mind the centre of gravity. It's useful to pile bags into the underside of the buggy, but you have to remember that the infant is then the only thing keeping the device level – as soon as you remove her, the buggy is going to tip backwards. This is highly amusing for anyone watching, but not for you – and is especially not fun if you have a sloping driveway.

Oh, and a pushchair is also supposed to be easy to collapse and store. It is, in the same way that a flat-pack shelf is easy to assemble within one hour using only a screwdriver. Expect a few fumbles and muttered curses before you get it right.

Chapter 13
Take Me Out

27% of British households do not have access to a car or van, according to the Office of National Statistics.

bviously your lives can't stop and you will have to go on a journey with the children in tow at some point. As with a lot of things, how smoothly this goes depends on the preparation and the management.

Driving me mad

If you are the kind of person whose car is their pride and joy, it may be time to take a reality check and trade down for something more battered. Your sparkling Peugeot or Sierra isn't going to stay that way with a small person on board. Babies don't discriminate – they'll barf over the furnishings of a brand new BMW just as easily as over a battered old Ford Escort.

Children in cars need *entertaining*. This doesn't mean you need to have a built-in PlayStation and satellite TV/DVD unit built into the back of the driver's seat (whatever some car manufacturers may like you to believe). In my experience, hilarity can be induced by the front-seat passenger simply pushing a soft toy above the head-rest for the entertainment of the back-seat passengers. Repeatedly.

Obviously you don't want to spend the entire journey auditioning for *The Sooty Show*, so you may need to find other ways of keeping them happy. Rattles, little toys that play tunes and so on are all right for a while for smaller passengers, but toddlers and pre-schoolers will need a bit more: some colouring books and crayons are a good bet, and you can make small 'treats' go a long way. If you don't fancy stuffing them full of sweets to keep them quiet and you want something healthier, a bag of grapes in the front, offered one at a time, can be a good idea (for children over three – grapes can be a choking hazard for younger ones).

Do not, on any account, allow them to have one of their music tapes/CDs on in the car. That way lies madness.

The wheels on the bus

Taking your child on a bus gets easier the more you do it. First of all, you have to become immune to the reactions of other passengers, which will probably include stares, scowls, tuts and heartfelt sighs at how long it's taking you to bounce the buggy up to the level of the bus. Deep down, several people will be thinking, 'Please, please don't sit *that* next to me.'

You will spend the journey praying that your child does not make an embarrassing comment about any of your fellow passengers. When my daughter was three, she and I once found ourselves sitting on the tram opposite a man with a shaven head and extensive facial tattoos. She turned to me and intoned in her usual stage-whisper: 'Daddy, does that man *need* drawing on his face?'

Luckily, he turned out to be amused and we had a laugh about it. Thankful to have got off lightly, we decided that we would not be so lucky next time, and that we would try to see such comments coming and forestall them.

The following week, Daughter and Mum were on the bus and, predictably, Daughter found herself staring at a young woman with multiple piercings, including a ring through her lip and a collection of small rivets peppering her face like silver acne. 'Mummy,' she began, 'that lady …' My wife, quick as a flash, distracted her with a biscuit and started talking about something else. Daughter was not to be so easily put off. She tried again, her voice indistinct through layers of half-chewed biscuit. "Mummy, that lady's got ...' My wife began talking very loudly. 'Do you want to do some painting when we get home? Yes, let's do that.' And so it went on. Through a combination of ingenuity, interruption and simply drowning her out, the embarrassing observations were deflected. As they got off the bus, leaving the multi-pierced woman deep in her magazine and unaware that anything was amiss, my daughter was heard to wail plangently: 'Mummy, I was only going to *say*, that lady's got a nice stripey top like mine.'

To get back to the point, children on public transport are, like children in restaurants, tolerated rather than encouraged, and for the same reasons – i.e. they take up a space without bringing in revenue. In most parts of the UK you can take your children free on public transport until they are five years old. This must be a sore point with bus company operators whose sole purpose is to bring in as much profit as possible while keeping the service at a just-tolerable level of shoddiness.

In advertising circles, they do research into 'consumer resistance', trying to predict things like exactly how much you can shave off the size of a chocolate bar before customers will start to notice and decide that it's not very good value any more. This principle applies to public transport as well. If you are a company with a monopoly on a particular route, there's no point investing in brand new, smooth-running buses with comfortable seats and clean windows, when these extra standards aren't going to bring in any additional custom. So we're saying (a) enjoy the free travel for under-5s, because it may not last, and (b) you may as well support your local bus route – because it isn't going to get any better, but it may, if people don't use it, get worse or be taken off altogether. You may not be bothered about that now if you have your family safely ensconced in a 4×4 (SUV) for any journey longer than a hundred yards – but one day, your clutch may go just as you're getting ready to set off to see Auntie Mabel or to catch a train, and so you may just find that the Number 33 comes in handy.

Parent & Toddler parking spaces

The special Parent & Toddler spaces located near to the shop entrance have extra wide bits either side of where you park the car. They exist for a reason. They are there so that your four-year-old driver doesn't prang the nearby Mercedes while trying to reverse into the space. Just kidding. They are there so that people like us can set up the pushchair, haul the child or children out of the car, get them strapped in and shut the car door safely – without having to place a child in the path of a thundering juggernaut while you do this.

Oddly, some people read the sign 'Parent & Toddler Spaces' and think that it actually says 'Free Spaces For Anybody'.

Remember that the provision of these spaces is not a legal right, and is probably little more than a public relations exercise on the part of the supermarkets. But they *are* there, and they're provided for you and your child. Stand firm if you see any Not-We using these. There's nothing wrong with going up to someone and giving a polite reminder about who the spaces are actually for – they probably would not abuse a disabled space in the same way, after all. The Militant Wing of the New Parent brigade sometimes recommends giving the registration number to the shop's Customer Service Desk.

Bear in mind that it's in their interests to leave the spaces available for us. Believe me, if you're getting a little wriggler out of the car when you're parked in a normal space, it's all too easy for their flailing feet to catch the wing-mirror or the paintwork of the neighbouring car. And then who'll be moaning?

Give it a few months and you'll be on the Parent & Toddler parking space barricades, defending them to the last man.[1]

Food for thought

The UK is renowned – if that's the word – for being the *most child-unfriendly* nation in Europe. When it comes to tolerance of children in public places and catering for their needs, the British are lagging far behind their European neighbours. Certainly if you have spent any time in France, Spain or Italy, where children are not only tolerated but welcomed and celebrated as part of the family experience, you'll have noted a marked contrast with attitudes in the UK – or rather, England specifically. Sarah Tucker, in her book *Have Toddler Will Travel* (Hodder, 2002), gives England a paltry three out of ten for its attitude towards toddlers (interestingly, Wales, Scotland, Ireland and especially the Isle of Man rate rather more highly).

As a new parent, you'll have been on the other side of the fence not so long ago, and, as with the pushchair issue, you can probably see both sides. If you've gone out with your beloved for a little intimate meal *à deux*, you don't want this to be disrupted by someone's two-year-old screaming at full volume and throwing bits of sausage around.[2]

If an establishment advertises itself as 'family-friendly', we enter into a contract. We will not let our children run amok, bang on the tables and upturn the furniture; we make every effort to

---

1 As the old joke goes, a conservative is just a liberal who's been mugged.
2 Unless you are still trying to dissuade your wife or girlfriend from starting a family, of course, in which case it's probably a very effective idea.

discipline them and make sure they behave and eat in a manner not likely to offend other diners. In return, the establishment makes us feel welcome, and not just served through gritted teeth with one eye on the clock. It's no coincidence that so many people choose to stop at the likes of Little Chef on long journeys, despite the quick-fix cuisine – it's one place you can be sure children are welcome and given their own menu and some crayons and something to colour, and where there will be an abundance of high-chairs. Either restaurants want our money, in which case they put up with families' foibles (and that includes children getting a little restless, and toddlers who sometimes cry), or they put a big sign on the door to tell us that kids aren't welcome – which they have every right to do – and we will take our money somewhere else.

The sea change in attitudes, as far as it has gone, has happened in our lifetime. In my parents' day, pubs were not geared up to catering for children. Some landlords were still doing a lot of brow-furrowing and head-scratching over the notion of letting women in. And their idea of a varied menu was a choice between cheese and onion or salt and vinegar. Let's be honest – young families eating out are now a strong market for pub catering, and as long as this continues to be the case, you'll find places which offer food for children, either the usual scampi and chips and ice-creams or, if you are lucky, something a little more inventive.

Having said all that, there is *surely* still a gap in the market for a restaurant chain which welcomes all ages and doesn't patronize its patrons? One which acknowledges that some of us would like to sit down with our children on proper chairs, at a proper wooden (not plastic) table, with proper knives and forks? One where we can choose healthy and inexpensive dishes made with fresh ingredients (not reheated) from a proper menu (without the need for pictures)? Where the children's menu offers something slightly more imaginative than chicken nuggets, sausages or pizza? Where children's options are graded in size (and price) according to age, rather than being the catch-all 'child's portion' intended to serve everybody from a picky two-year-old to a ravenous teenager?

Over to you.

Come as you are

At some point in your child's first year, there will come the joyous occasion of the first social event to which you are invited as a family. Your first reaction may be, 'Oh, God, Lucinda and Miles have invited us to their wedding and they don't have kids. What are we going to do?' (To which your wife will respond, 'Lucinda and who?')

Seriously, the first thing to do is check that your darling son or daughter is actually invited and welcome. There's nothing worse than turning up at a wedding and finding that you don't have room for all of you at the table. You won't need a place setting for your little one if they're still on the jars or the home-made mash, but it would be nice to know you have space to squeeze the pushchair in between you and the bride's university friend's boyfriend.

If Baby is welcome, then you're fine – everyone will want to come up to you and tell you how cute she is. On the other hand, you don't want to steal the bride's thunder, so be diplomatic. As for christenings, they are always full of screaming kids, so you won't have anything to worry about there.

With everything, though, the key is in the preparation. You can't allow for every contingency, but at least you know you'll have done everything possible if you have a well-stocked changing bag to hand (complete with good supplies of nappies, wipes, nappy-sacks, cream and changes of clothing), plus appropriate foodstuffs and entertainment items.

Distraction is the thing. The last thing you want at a wedding is for your child to be the one who pipes up after the priest intones: 'And if anyone should know of any just cause or impediment …'

Interlude: Don't try this with your children, even if you are tempted

Police in Radnor, Pennsylvania, interrogated a suspect by placing a metal colander on his head and connecting it with wires to a photocopying machine. The message 'HE'S LYING' was placed in the copier, and police pressed the 'Copy' button every time they thought the suspect wasn't telling the truth. Believing the 'lie detector' to be real, the suspect confessed.

Chapter 14
Pump Up the Volume

Mothers featured in *Guardian* article about working parents
in February 2005: *eight*
Fathers featured in *Guardian* article about working parents
in February 2005: *none*

hakespeare called midnight 'the very witching time of night', but that's nothing. Midnight is for wimps. Try two, three, or even what Mike Oldfield inexplicably referred to in 'Moonlight Shadow' as '4 a.m. in the morning'. Try it when there's nothing you want to do but sleep and you are downstairs in the company of a small, exuberant person who wants to run around, play and watch those repeats with the sign-language interpreter bobbing around in front – until the birds start singing in the trees outside.

It's the one thing everyone tells you. The thing they all think they know about children. *Have kids and you'll never sleep again*. It's impossible to generalize, though. You hear stories of parents who did not have a full night's sleep from the day their child was born until he was five. These people are the ultimate baby martyrs; they look permanently exhausted, but, somehow, still achieve a kind of Zen serenity. It's as if they have passed through stress and insanity and have come out the other side, into some transcendental dimension reserved only for parents who have experienced the living hell of the Permanent Screamer.

It's equally possible that you'll seethe with envy listening to the mums and dads whose little darlings sleep with no problems at all through every single night. This is sometimes because they have been 'doing Gina', an expression that you will come to hate. (Not some illicit stimulant, but rather the globally successful *Contented Little Baby* plan put forward by Gina Ford, in which your baby eats, sleeps and defecates to order, down to the last minute – and probably grows up to be a dictator.)

You will, eventually, want to kill these people. The only way to stop yourself is to keep hoping that yours will recompense you later in life. You pray they will turn into teenagers who want to slouch in their beds until noon at weekends, giving you a good four hours a day without your having to attend to their needs – and that the lie-abed toddlers will become fit, sporty types who demand to be conveyed to freezing running tracks and sports pitches at six in the morning every Saturday.

If at first you don't get heard, cry cry again
When you see a cartoon of a baby, it's usually got a wobbling speech-balloon with something in it approximating to 'WAAAAAAA!' This is rubbish. Nobody who has ever listened to a child's cry can think it sounds remotely like 'WAAAAAAA!' It's more insidious than that, something on the edge of words which begins with a labial L or a U, more like 'Luuuuuuuuur' or even 'uuuuuuuaaahhh-uaaahhh!'

Often, it will mutate mid-scream into either a 'Daaaaaaa!' or a 'Maaaaaa!' Couples lie awake at night, cold and rigid, each of them listening out for that first tell-tale consonant so that they can kick the other, saying 'She wants *you*,' and then roll over in a meaningful 'I'm going back to sleep' kind of way.

Most parents operate a system of turns when it comes to getting up to attend to Baby's needs – although if the little one is breastfeeding, you may get off lightly by virtue of not having the required tools.

Also, as a man, you will find yourself able to do something which women claim men can do and women cannot – namely, sleep through the sound of your baby's cries. Of course, this will depend how tired you are, how hard you have been working and how far the baby's room is from yours, but you can make the most of fitting in with your stereotype. Good luck.

The cry can mean any number of things depending on the situation – here are just a number of possible translations for a baby aged under 18 months. Context is everything – you'll usually manage to work out which one it is.

- 'I wish to partake of nutritious warm milk – please supply forthwith!'
- 'I wish to belch. Please pick me up and pat me on the back.'
- 'Do you realize I have been sitting in my own fecal matter for the past half-hour and it is starting to become a biohazard threatening the entire area? Please decontaminate!'
- 'Look, I am bored with my cot and would like to spend a few hours in your bed, lying at right angles to you and kicking you in the back/balls/head. Please come and get me.'
- 'My teddy has fallen down the back of the cot and this is obviously the biggest tragedy known to mankind.'
- 'Have you seen this interesting stain on the sheet? I wonder if you could come and ascertain for me whether it's chocolate or something more challenging.'
- 'You let my afternoon nap go on for too long today, probably while you were flat out on the sofa watching *Cagney And Lacey*. Now I'm not tired. Ha!'
- 'I want to go downstairs and watch the 3 a.m. repeat of *Panorama* with that funny little man waving his arms about in front of it.'

- 'You've actually been getting a bit of sleep recently, so I want to make sure you are suitably exhausted for that meeting tomorrow.'
- 'I want to embarrass you and annoy your neighbours.'
- 'I just wanted to remind you I was still here.'
- 'I just really want to annoy you.'
- All of the above.

Extreme noise terror
Maybe you'll empathize with these quotes from first-time dads:

- 'The worst time is when they cry. You just feel you can't do anything, and even that what you are doing is making it worse. It's an awful feeling, that this little person is distressed and you can't do anything about it.'
- 'We just needed to get away from the crying, to be honest. I had to put her down in her cot, close the door and walk away for a few minutes, or I would just have gone mad.'
- 'When we first got him home from hospital, he seemed to do nothing but cry. We'd make sure he was fed, changed and winded, but it carried on and on and on. We just reached the conclusion that he enjoyed tormenting us.'
- 'We'd cuddle her for a bit, put her back in the cot and sneak out of the room. Then you might breathe too loudly, or a floorboard would creak or something and she'd start crying all over again. It just seemed like a never-ending cycle.'

No sleep till …
One thing which sometimes works is taking the child into your bed. This is fine as far as it goes, but it does mean two things:

some Aerosmith cranked up to 11. You may laugh, but some babies seem to enjoy nodding off to sleep to the rhythms of really loud rock music. (My little boy used to love doing this to 'Since You've Been Gone' by Rainbow. I bet Ritchie Blackmore never thought he was creating a lullaby.)

- They don't look very aesthetically pleasing. Who wants to see a child with a piece of plastic shoved in his mouth?

- A dummy can impede early development of speech, and they have also been linked to ear infections.

- Back to the British Dental Association, who can't seem to make up their minds: 'If your child sucks its thumb or on a dummy for long periods, it could cause problems in the way the teeth develop. The pressure of the dummy or thumb against the back of the teeth could push them forward, which may mean your child will need corrective treatment later on.'

- It can be hard to get them off it – along with nappies, crawling and not using cutlery, the dummy is just one more 'baby habit' to get your child out of, and it's an optional one. At some point, they will have to give it up – maybe it's simpler just never to have had it in the first place. As the saying goes, if they've never had it, they won't miss it. Worth remembering that it presumably didn't do our great-grandmothers any harm not to be dummied at every opportunity.

- *What you shouldn't say to an anti-dummy parent*: 'She screams quite loudly, doesn't she? Have you thought about using a dummy?'

Anyway, if you want some sensible grown-up advice on this, you could do a lot worse than have a look here:
www.babyworld.co.uk/features/dummy.htm

Chapter 16
Eat to the Beat

According to the Infant and Dietetic Foods Association (IDFA), *10% of mothers* 'encounter difficulties in weaning their child onto solid foods'. (Strangely, the IDFA does not report how many fathers do.)

I n recent years, attempts have been made to spice up *baby food* (sometimes literally), giving rise to a whole range of exotic flavours on the supermarket shelves. Baby's Beef Fricassée, Baby's Chicken Cacciatore with Focaccia, Toddler's Prawn Madras with Naan and Onion Bhaji … All right, so I'm exaggerating a bit, but you get the idea.

Meanwhile, whole books are devoted to recipes for one-year-olds which are as complex and time-consuming as the average Jamie Oliver dish for a six-person dinner party. These books inhabit an alternative universe. They usually feature air-brushed Stepford Infants, their clean bibs neatly fixed around their scrubbed faces, beaming beatifically as they contemplate a colour-coordinated spread of avocado dip with bruschetta sticks and organic tomato salad.

Now, we know otherwise. We know that it will have taken a lot of time and effort – and possibly bribing with chocolate – to get them looking that immaculate. We know that, in reality, much of the plate's contents will end up on the small customer's face, a lot more will land on the floor and what remains will simply be spread across the plate in an artistic manner (maybe after being chewed experimentally). So don't these attempts to turn the middle-class infant's diet into five-star cuisine seem … ambitious? Someone of a cynical bent might even suggest that the purpose of these concoctions is to sell cookbooks, the writers never having any serious ideas about parents actually trying the recipes out. Oh-ho. They might say that, and I couldn't possibly comment.

Let's face it, your average toddler (him again), on being presented with a butternut squash purée accompanied by zucchini fingers, isn't going to think, 'Oooh, parent, you are spoiling me!' He's going to think, 'Yippee – brightly-coloured ammo!' And you will duck.

That's not to say you can't get them to eat healthily, of course – but you can do so very simply and cheaply and without having to resort to an expensive 'lifestyle' recipe book. It's not as if your toddler is going to start hosting dinner parties just yet. Repeat after me: *these books exist to make you feel inadequate.*

Ready, steady, chuck

Whether you feed your children such elaborate recipes or whether you give them fish fingers with spaghetti hoops, you'll still end up down on your hands and knees trying to pick bits of dried food out of the carpet.

And a word of warning – some of the residue can be danger-ous. It is actually possible to *cut yourself on Weetabix*. Yes, I too would have laughed at this suggestion five years ago, but believe me, it is a deadly serious matter. Just a small trace of Weetabix, when left to become encrusted on the side of a table, can turn grit-hard – and if you attempt to remove it with the standard issue wipe or damp piece of kitchen roll, it can cut the skin of your forefinger and leave you bleeding copiously. I speak from experience. Of such stories are books about bizarre household accidents made.

You can get very frustrated if, during attempts at weaning, most of what you are trying to feed them ends up on the floor. One of the most sensible pieces of advice we were given on this is not to look at their food intake on a day-to-day basis, but over a period of a week or even a month. Doing this, you get a far more realistic idea of what they are actually eating – and usually, a far more positive one.

We're s-h-o-p-p-i-n-g

Baby food jars come in all shapes and sizes. Luckily, all the shapes are usually irrelevant and all the sizes relate to the age for which they are appropriate, which is always marked on the side of the jar.

As a rule, you shouldn't buy ahead of your child's age – but you can backdate quite happily. A 12-monther's lamb casserole is suitable for that age because it has more chunky bits suitable for someone with teeth, and as such it's not going to be any good for a six-monther. On the other hand, our daughter was quite happily guzzling the pure fruit purées and the smooth vanilla puddings intended for four-monthers right up to her first birthday, alongside the more filling fare which she was getting used to. She just liked them. It's a question of finding out what's suitable for your own child, which you usually manage to do by trial and error.

This, however, will not prevent you from falling into that trap laid for the unwary dad – no, it will not save you from that heinous crime known as *Getting The Wrong Thing*.

You will be bound to Get The Wrong Thing at least once. When you come back from the supermarket with bags of baby food or ingredients, the statistical likelihood is that you will have got 97% Right Stuff and 3% Wrong Stuff. In most examinations, 97% is a score which would have your teacher bouncing off the ceiling with delight. You will usually even have bought the right size of nappies, which should in itself be cause for celebration and joy.

Not so. Your other half will ignore all the Right Stuff which you've bought and will pick out, between thumb and forefinger usually, the Wrong Thing. Let's say it's a jar of lamb and cauliflower 'casserole' – actually a brownish mush, indistinguishable from the rest of the brownish mush which goes in one end of your child (and from that which comes out of the other, frankly).

'Why? Have you? Bought this?' she will ask. Just like that, with three question marks strategically placed in the sentence, all backing each other up in case one gets away.

You think of the various possible answers. You ponder, 'You sent me out to get food,' but you sense – rightly – that this is not quite homing in on the exact nuance of her question.

'Well, um … he had it before.'
'He had it before and he didn't like it. He scrunched up his face and spat it everywhere. Don't you *remember*?'

You think about this one. The intended recipient of this gourmet meal is a small toddler. Scrunching up his face and spitting it everywhere is something you tend to associate, if you are honest, with most of the things you have ever tried to shovel into his unwilling mouth. Especially those which involve vegetables. It hasn't occurred to you that there are actual grades of preference when it comes to baby food.

'Well, maybe he can try it again. He might like it this time.'

You seize on something she has said herself, only a few days ago.

'We're supposed to be getting him used to new tastes and textures.'
'Yes, but he *doesn't like lamb*.'
'Well, sorry. I've bought it now.'

She shrugs and then makes that dangerous hissing noise from between her teeth, before gingerly placing the jar alongside the others in the food cupboard. 'All right. But he won't like it.'
He doesn't like it, of course. And you end up wiping it off the walls.

Oh, and the average child takes 18 tastings of a new food to get used to it. So start them early on the chicken vindaloo.

Interlude: Scene from a dispute

*'Right, that's it. If you do that again,
I'm taking your Disney cards away for a week.'
'But you can't!'
'I can, young lady, and I will.'
'No – you caaaaan't!'
'Give me one good reason why I can't.'
'Because you took them away yesterday.'*

Chapter 17
Moving On Up

'The man who is to gain a living by his labour must be drawn away from home, or at least from the cradleside, to perform that labour; but this will not, if he be made of good stuff, prevent him from doing his share of the duty due to his children.'

William Cobbett (1830)

 t some point, you may feel like doing one of your own checklists to challenge those you find in the official parenting manuals – something like this.

The 22nd month
By now, your child *should be able to*:

- Whine incessantly, especially if favourite toy is taken away or favourite video turned off, or while being strapped into pushchair.
- Clamp teeth tightly shut when having them cleaned, thus preventing access to back teeth.
- Attempt to secrete toy cars and/or Lego bricks about person, usually in nappy region or mouth.
- Liberally smear clothes and hair with food stains.

… will probably be able to:

- Twist and kick violently while having nappy changed, so as to cause maximum mess and inconvenience.
- Hurl shoes a distance of at least 2 metres (6 feet).

- Scatter semi-liquid food on floor and secrete chunks of mouldering banana down side of booster seat.
- Respond to every instruction with 'No!'

... *may possibly be able to*:

- Inflict physical injury on another child (with implements).
- Twist head from side to side when having teeth cleaned, so that toothpaste ends up largely all over face and not in mouth.
- Pull books, CDs and videos from shelves and scatter all over floor and beneath furniture.

... *may even be able to*:

- Inflict physical injury on another child (without implements).
- Cause irreparable damage to stairgate, shower curtain or chest of drawers.
- Insert slices of freshly buttered toast (with jam) into slot of video-recorder, causing permanent damage.
- Drive father/mother to seek vasectomy/sterilization as appropriate, rather than risk going through all this again.

The long game

Parenting is an unfair sport. Just as you feel you have a grasp of the rules and you're heading speedily down the wing towards an open goal, somebody not only moves the goalposts but informs you that you're actually supposed to have been playing cricket all the time. And then they tie your shoelaces together and knee you in the groin.

Up until now, you may have been slowly winning your war of attrition against Baby Devastation. You may even have felt, after three or four months, that you were getting into some sort of routine and you kind of knew what you were doing by instinct rather than having to look it up in a book, or ask the health visitor all the time. But a seismic shift comes when Baby transforms those rolls across the floor into something more directional – and now she is learning how to crawl. At the time, you're delighted. You may want to video it, ring people up to tell them about it, post it on the Internet and write it in the sky in clouds. Baby will look up at you with a disparaging, even disgusted expression on her face, as if to say, 'Dad, you're so embarrassing.' (This will be the natural state of things for the next twenty-one years or so.)

It will dawn on you, some time around the eight-month mark, that what you have now in the house is an entirely different species. Someone has taken away your small, cute, chubby person who usually did nothing more exciting than lie on the playmat, wave his arms and legs and gurgle (and occasionally spray you with poo). Now, your child can crawl. This makes him dangerous.

It is a major lifestyle step for Baby. In many ways, it has a lot in common with the point at which an eighteen-year-old passes his driving test and suddenly wants to borrow the car every night to go out to suspicious sounding gigs with odd-looking Marilyn Manson-type friends.

And so it begins.

Chapter 18
Walking On Sunshine

Another inevitable truth: You can childproof your home. But it won't make any difference. They will still get in.

t happens gradually. Now crawling, she starts to haul herself up by whatever means are available: book-shelves, Dad's trouser leg, table leg, stairgate, bath … Anything at all to get to the vertical. And she's off.

In just a few weeks she has developed what the books call 'cruise control'. This is a kind way of saying the following. Up until now, you have had to put up with someone who can scream at window-shattering volume and hit the wall at three feet with a well-aimed bowel movement, but over whom you had one major tactical advantage, namely your mobility – and now, suddenly, your adversary has caught up with you. It's like that bit in *Superman 2* when the temporarily Super-powerless Clark Kent has a run-in with a belligerent guy in a bar, and he gets prop-erly thumped for the first time in his life. It's as if they've called in the cavalry. You now have to share your house with a small, demented vandal and hooligan *who can travel*.

The toddler now arriving

Nothing is safe any more. You remove all breakable objects. Even placing them on higher shelves is no guarantee of safety, because the really inventive toddler can reach up with one of those funny rubber sticks that go *boing* and knock the vase of flowers on to the floor. They will do anything to get round bar-riers put in their way. Some examples of toddler determination show an inventiveness which you can only admire, such as the boy who built a small set of steps out of his books in order to climb over the stairgate which was impeding his path. You just know he'll go far.

So, there it is – you need to adapt your life again, and become skilled at ducking, diving, and simply running away. Some people consider it prudent at this point to fit child proof locks on to the cupboard doors. You can also affix rounded edges to any sharp-edged tables, dressers, etc., although some parents just go with the flow and let children learn that running full tilt into a hard wooden surface is going to hurt. Stairgates are a useful addition too, although you'll find they will effectively impede any adult visitors from getting upstairs to the bathroom as well.

Oh, and once toddlers have gained confidence in walking, they don't just walk – they seem to *run* everywhere, sprinting from room to room as if they have to get a certain number of tasks done within a time limit. You let them do this, because anything that tires them out is good news. And when they get to about the age of three, they are very useful for fetching you magazines, glasses, etc. from the other room.

Of course, the downside is that they can just disappear where they want, when they feel like it. So lock and bolt all outside doors. And if that doesn't work, consider getting them electronically tagged.

Talk talk
There is a story about the famous scientist and all-round clever person Albert Einstein, which all parents would do well to remember.

Young Albert, apparently, didn't say a single word as a baby or toddler. In fact, he didn't say anything for his first four years. Naturally his parents started to get very worried and had him referred to all kinds of specialists, to no avail. Then, one day, out of the blue, little Albert came out with his first utterance, the fully-formed sentence: 'This soup is too hot!' After they had got over their general rejoicing and relief, Herr and Frau Einstein turned to Albie and said: 'But why have you not spoken, up to now?' The boy shrugged and said: *'Bis jetzt, alles in Ordnung.'*

(Which, roughly translated, means: 'Well, up to now every-thing's been OK.')

People may think you are mad for talking to something which doesn't answer back, but how else is he going to learn to speak? Everything in Baby's little world has a name, so there's nothing wrong with giving him a running commentary on everything you do right from the start. Of course, this will make you appear totally bonkers to the Not-We, but then you should have come to expect that by now. It'll all be worth it when you first hear something back.

It's a funny old game. You spend two years teaching them how to walk and talk, and the next sixteen telling them to sit down and shut up.

Interlude: Advice from one child to another

'When your dad is cross with you and he asks, "Do I look stupid?" he doesn't really want you to answer.'

Chapter 19
What Have I Done to Deserve This?

toddler *n.* a child who is just beginning to walk.

 f course, there's rather more to it than the above dictionary definition would suggest. *Is your child a toddler?* Take our simple quiz to find out.

1 Your hosts offer him some food which he's not that keen on. What does he do?
   a) Murmurs, 'Sorry, I'm not all that hungry.'
   b) Eats it anyway, just to be polite.
   c) Screws up his face, spits out his mouthful, turns the plate upside down and tips the contents across the floor while banging the plate on the table.

2 She is very tired. How is she most likely to react?
   a) Yawn and stretch.
   b) Make a nice cup of cocoa and lie down with a good book.
   c) Stamp, scream and shout, rubbing her eyes and wailing.

3 In the supermarket queue, she is bored and fed up. What does she do?
   a) Smiles sweetly and asks you what you are cooking tonight.
   b) Smiles at the cashier or other people in the queue.
   c) Grabs items from the trolley and tries to gnaw them open, before throwing them to the floor while stamping, screaming and crying.

4   A friend wants to borrow one of his possessions. What is his
likely reaction?
a) He will lend it to them happily.
b) He will let them keep it.
c) He will snarl and scream, while clutching the item to his
chest and systematically beating the friend around the
head with his fist.

5   What does he think of the Teletubbies?
a) They're just harmless fun.
b) They are quite boring, really.
c) 'Aaaaaahhh! Uh-oh, uh-oh! 'Gain-'gain-'gain!!'

6   While eating, she accidentally spills some food down her
front. How does she deal with this?
a) She surreptitiously sponges it off.
b) She becomes embarrassed and apologizes profusely.
c) She laughs loudly, making sure everyone is looking at
her, before smearing the stain up her clothes and into her
face and hair.

7   When undertaking a relaxing afternoon trip to the park with
the children, what do you need to take?
a) Nothing.
b) Wallet or purse.
c) Four changes of underwear, a packet of antibacterial
wipes, sun-cream, six toys (at least one of which must
go 'beep'), two changes of clothes, several packets of
snacks, a large wipe-clean book and sturdy land-trans-
port.

8 How does your child normally make friends with people?
  a) Enjoying a shared hobby or interest.
  b) Saying hello over the garden fence.
  c) Running up to them, making a noise like a seagull and hitting them repeatedly with a stuffed furry octopus.

9 What is your child's preferred activity on a long car journey?
  a) Sleeping.
  b) Enjoying the scenery.
  c) Kicking the back of the seat, spilling fruit juice over himself, whining 'when wc bo *deeeeere?*' squashing raisins into the space behind the door handle and wanting to stop every half-hour to go to the toilet.

10 When meeting someone at a social gathering for the first time, what does your child do?
  a) Politely asks their name.
  b) Smiles and offers to get them a drink.
  c) Pulls down his trousers and shows his bottom, before telling them that they are very fat and asking if they want to see his *Stuart Little* video, then crying when they say no.

Give yourself one *toddler point* for every question to which you answered (c).

If you scored more than three, you *definitely have a toddler*.

Chapter 20
Semi-detached Suburban Mr James

one-upmanship *n. colloq*. The act of gaining or maintaining a psychological advantage.

ou and your significant other will possibly acquire new 'friends' after the baby is born, people with whom the only thing you have in common is the fact that they, too, have just had a small and squealing person emerge into the world.

This is a remarkably tenuous basis on which to found a friendship. You wouldn't necessarily expect to socialize with someone because they like the same brand of baked beans as you, or drive the same car. Even supporting the same football team isn't always a safe bet. So, this is the point at which you apply some common sense. If they seem like the kind of people you'd normally want to be friends with, then fine. But if not, *run a mile*. Your real friends will have children soon enough, if they haven't already. It just isn't worth enduring social anguish, subtle competitiveness and endless conversations about nothing in particular just on the off-chance that they may be able to give you some weaning tips, or help you form a babysitting circle.

Here is a brief guide to some mums and dads you may have to meet in the course of your socialising, and how to deal with them.

1   Alpha Mum

Some odd, Stepford Wife transformation seems to have come over her. Because she lives in (what she considers to be) a desirable part of suburbia and has a hubby who does (what she considers to be) an admirably manly job, she has a veneer of self-confidence and arrogance which makes you want to douse her with a bucket of cold water. Watch Alpha Mum's subtle jockeying for supremacy at Sunday afternoon gatherings: the snubs with the merest turn of an elbow, the marking of territory by simply placing a baby in front of a particular toy, the subtle criticism of one child simply by praising two or three of the others. Desmond Morris would have a field day. Hubby, meanwhile, is off playing away with his secretary. She knows, and pretends it's not happening.

2   Windsock Mum

Devoid of any particularly interesting personality traits herself, her trick is to latch on to whoever is dominant that week and suck up to them, laughing at their useless jokes and praising their child. Changes allegiances faster than Britney Spears changes her image. Always laughs rather too loudly, offers to make rather too many cups of tea and is the first to get her diary out at the end of the afternoon, desperate to meet again.

3   Sports Dad

Will be getting everyone out in the garden playing cricket when they'd much rather be putting their feet up with a cup of tea. Makes sure that he enrols his child – boy or girl – for football training sessions as soon as possible and makes them watch every sporting event on TV. Will also try to engage you in complicated manly discussions about defence tactics, possibly using toys as props.

4   Hyper-Career Mum

Has a prestigious job, probably in the Civil Sevice, and considers the rest of the group to be beneath her. Her nostrils always seem to be flaring in slight disgust, as if she can permanently smell something offensive. She will run for school governor as something to put on her CV – in fact, her application to be a governor will look very like a career resumé itself, complete with smart photo. Usually, any attempt to engage her in conversation will be futile – she will just give you a monosyllabic answer before turning away and addressing something to the Competitive Mum on the other side of the room.

5   Car Dad

Will inevitably open the conversation with, 'So what are you driving these days?' and will think it hilarious if you reply, 'Um, a car,' or, 'Nothing, we came by bus.' He reminds you of that guy who was going to go on *Mastermind* with the topic 'Routes To Anywhere In Mainland Britain By Road', and he will get the road atlas out at the slightest provocation. If he has a boy, then the youngster will already be trained to read the names on the back of cars and to know the spec of different makes. Little does he know that his son harbours a secret desire to be a ballet dancer.

6   Social Climber Mum

Considers herself to be a cut above the rest because she has managed to secure her nirvana, a house in the most sought-after street of the most desirable school catchment in the city. She talks down her council estate origins and never misses an opportunity to flash her *nouveau riche* credentials, a sort of metaphorical bling. Her husband's money has bought her a veneer of style and middle-class respectability. A more smug face you never did see.

7 Unreconstructed Dad

Jokes – but in such a way as to convey that it's perfectly true – that he doesn't know where the washing machine is and that he couldn't hoover to save his life. You already know this, because his wife has told yours about it at great length. When his wife came home with the new baby, he was to be found staring into the cupboards and complaining that there was no food. The idea that he might change a nappy is about as likely as the idea that he might breastfeed.

8 Loud Mum

Permanently on Transmit. Her child is the centre of the Universe, and if your child has done something, Loud Mum's infant will have done it a month earlier. If you've been on holiday to Thailand, Loud Mum will have done that before it was fashionable and is currently planning a family trip to the Moon. She is also one of those people who think they can be as rude as they like, without ever bothering about the consequences. When discussing cots, she refers in a faux-inverted-snobbery way to 'some cheap wooden thing from John Lewis.' Her four bedroom house is not good enough for her and as she has no intention of living in a 'boring semi like everyone else', she has badgered hubby to buy a Gothic, phallic monstrosity of a converted clock tower from which she holds court.

Remember: it's good for your kids to play with as diverse a mix of little friends as you can find – but not at cost to your own sanity. Life's too short to pretend to like people.

Chapter 21
See Emily Play

First rule of toys: *They don't have to be new.*

t's amazing how many parents will rush out and get their children the latest piece of polished metal or plastic which they've seen advertised. Children's TV is peppered with ads: plugs for tartrazine-and-sugar concoctions, cereals which look like dog food, tie-ins to TV shows and dolls which, unaccountably and disturbingly, have realistic genitals and practise lifelike acts of undinism. Marketing people with ponytails and red braces even have a name for the pressure children exert over their parents to become part of this great consumerist nightmare. They call it Pester Power. *Yeuch*.

Here's some news – up until the age of at least seven, kids aren't bothered about designer labels, who's got the newest toy or whether it's tied into the latest movie release. You can buy them stuff in sales, from fairs and fêtes and charity shops. *It doesn't matter*. Say this mantra again and again: 'Spending money does not make me a good parent. Saving money does.'

Exceptions that prove the rule

Some things *are* worth buying new – videos and DVDs, for example, and anything where electrical or battery power is integral to the function of the thing. That's because, with these items, you can't really tell what the quality is like until you get it home. Videos could be stretched to snapping point, DVDs could be scratched, battery-powered cars could have their wheels soldered together with dried milk and old battery acid – and there's no consumer recourse if that's the case. But you can still look out for bargains. Buying birthday and Christmas presents in the sales doesn't make you stingy – it makes you shrewd.

And here's a tip, for if your child is looking at stuff on adverts and saying 'I want dat'. *Don't let them watch channels with adverts*. Or if that's not an option, you could only let them watch videos or DVDs you've chosen – that way, you'll know exactly what they are seeing.

See Chapter 34 for a more detailed low-down on today's TV for little ones.

Battlefield

Toddlers apply a very simple and rigid system of *rules* when playing with others. This is very easy to learn and understand and goes something like this:

- If I like the look of it – *mine*.
- If I'm holding it – *mine*.
- If I can take it off you – *mine*.
- If I was holding it just now – *mine*.
- If it looks a bit like one of mine – *mine*.
- If I'm bigger than you – *mine*.
- If it's in my house – *mine*.
- If it's in your house – *mine*.
- If I saw it first – *mine*.
- If you saw it first – *mine*.
- If you put it down for a second – *mine*.
- *And*: If it's broken, it's yours.

Toy decommissioning

People tend to be very generous when you have a baby: soft toys, rattles and clothes galore, if you're lucky. Birthdays and Christmas bring a slew of toys, many of which will be played with only once or twice before being heartlessly abandoned.

At this point, you have to take a long, hard look at your child's worldly goods and decide which ones they really need, and which ones would be more use at the local hospital, children's home or charity shop. Don't be sentimental about this – except when it comes to the teddies and the other chaps who share the cot, as they will almost be part of the family by now.

Swings and roundabouts

If the weather is fine and you want to get small children out of the house, then the one place you will always find yourself gravitating towards is the local playground. These vary enormously. Yours may be a state-of-the-art play paradise with wooden adventure-playground-style climbing equipment, gleaming swings and slides and an immaculate springy surface for safety. It is just as likely to be an eczematous patch of waste ground which doubles as a hangout for the local teenage junkies, sporting one broken slide, some flaking 'swing-bars' which look as if they haven't been painted since 1975 and an apologetic, creaking roundabout.

If you're lucky enough to have a good one nearby, you'll probably find it packed full of excitable children on Saturdays. Some have obviously been dumped there so that Mum can get on with the important business of smoking her cigarettes and reading *Heat* magazine. However, you'll find others full of parents whose watchfulness verges on the paranoid. There is a sort of unspoken rule that parents in playgrounds communicate through their children. 'Come on, Melissa, that little girl's waiting to get past.' Or: 'Cameron, mind that boy. Wait your turn.' You know the kind of thing. It seems especially true of dads.

Some, though, will even find themselves getting a touch competitive when it comes to sending little William or Oliver through the crawling tunnel. Parents in playgrounds have a veneer of politeness which hides their deep, fierce competitiveness – and dads with boys are the worst. It's inevitable. If that little chap in the red Next shirt has crossed the wobbly bridge without flinching and received a manly hug from his dad at the other end, then the last thing you want is for your own young man to stand on the brink, lip quivering, as a queue of rumbustious, impatient boys forms behind his quaking legs.

'Come on,' you say. 'You're holding everyone up.'

He shakes his head. The hand goes to the mouth and you know it's only going to be seconds before he bursts into tears. Quickly, you reach up and haul him down, smiling apologetically at Triumphant Dad and Next Boy. 'He's feeling a bit off colour today,' you say quickly. 'He prefers football, actually.'

Hurriedly, you lead him away to the swings, before you can catch the knowing smile from Triumphant Dad, who you know is secretly thinking, 'No, I bet he prefers dollies and fluffy bunnies, actually.'

Interlude: Conversations With My Daughter (1)

Me, to daughter on morning after England's Euro 2004 defeat by Portugal:
> *'England lost the football, Ellie.'*

Four-year-old tactical genius (after considered frown):
> *'Couldn't they find where it was?'*

Chapter 22
Don't Look Back In Anger

Average minutes per day which dads spent with children
in 1970s: *15*
Average minutes per day which dads spend with children
in 2000s: *180*

But would you ever let them go to the park on their own?

You'll find that you will never watch, read or listen to the news in quite the same way again. It's impossible to let stories of harm to children wash over you. It's not that you were heartless before, but if you were honest, it was filed under that heading of Terrible Things That Could Happen To Someone Else. Now, every story of child abuse or abduction will send a shiver through you; it's possible that you won't even be able to watch such things on the news. The media won't let the fact that such events are incredibly rare stand between them and a salacious story.

So we, today's parents, get teased for the fact that we drive children to school and don't like to let them go to the park unaccompanied. We are derided for taking them to friends' houses in the car when in our day we would have walked, ridden a bike, gone on roller skates, etc. The implication behind this is that we are letting children turn into a generation of indolent, fishy-pale slobs who baulk at the taste of fresh air, and that we are terrified to let them go out in case they are knocked down by a car or abducted by one of the leering child molesters who lurk in the bushes of every public space.

It's all very well for people to mock. To sneer that we wrap our children in cotton wool, that we are depriving them of the innocent pleasures of the great outdoors. After all, no more children are abducted today than 30 years ago – it's just that the media has raised its profile since the days when we, as primary school kids, were handed out bookmarks about 'stranger danger', featuring a picture of the Big Bad Wolf disguised as Little Red Riding Hood's granny.[1]

But, paranoia aside, there is more traffic on the roads these days, and there will be more roads to cross too. Your child is, statistically, far more likely to be hit by a car than abducted by a paedophile.

And here's another thing – families' greater mobility means that your child's best friend will not necessarily live round the corner, or even in the same town or village; it's just as likely that they live ten miles or even a hundred miles away. And it's also possible – and here we venture perhaps into heretical territory – that, when viewing our own childhood, the spectacles are of the Elton John circa 1974 variety, i.e. big and rose-tinted.

Nostalgia's not what it used to be

Look at the evidence. Some people of my generation would have you believe that we spent every Saturday afternoon haring recklessly down country lanes on Raleigh Chopper bikes while eating Marathon bars, before going off to ford streams, climb trees, scrump apples and annoy local pensioners until we got a 'clip round the ear' from the local bobby. We'd then alleg-

---

1   And these were just *terrifying* – certainly did the trick as far as I was concerned.

edly go off to play football in the street with an old tin-can until our mums called us in for tea. Yes, you can see the jerky, sun-kissed, brightly coloured cine-film footage and hear the seventies pop soundtrack. You can almost smell the bubblegum and taste the Fanta.

Except you can't. It's rubbish.

Quite probably, a lot of this is what Douglas Coupland cleverly refers to as 'legislated nostalgia'. People don't want to admit that their childhood actually *wasn't* like this, in case they go against the grain of the *I Love The Seventies*-style Jungian collective memory which has now come to replace actual recollection.

We airbrush out of our memories all the times when we sat inside on sunny afternoons playing cards or Connect Four, or annoyed our mums by moaning that there was 'nothing to doooo-ooo', or – perish the thought – *watched television*. And we may not have had PlayStations or Xboxes, but I'll bet a good few people of my age spent hours playing the adventure game *Hobbit* on the computer and wondering how to get through that bit with the barrels.[2] Or typing in every last semicolon of a BASIC game program from a magazine into their ZX-Spectrum or Commodore 64, only to have it crash after two minutes.

Yes, it's time we were honest. It is actually possible to convince yourself that you had a Raleigh Chopper bike even if you didn't. Some people who go misty-eyed at the mention of those sweets called Spangles may never actually have eaten them, and those who nod sagely and turn wistful at the words 'Bazooka Joe bubblegum' may never have bought any. Those talking heads on TV nostalgia shows who cheerfully recount the

---

2   You had to throw the barrel through the hatchway and then jump on top of it. Just in case you've been agonizing about this since you were thirteen.

times they turned their school uniform into full New Romantic gear and played truant to steal from the local record shop may not have done anything of the sort. But then, 'I was quite boring at school and I always did my homework on time' is not the kind of biography which your average C-list celeb wants to flaunt on prime-time TV.

It's possible that they *think* they did all these things, because these buzzwords, packaged images and hand-me-down ideas are so often invoked as totems of the past. It's part of the process of reinvention you undergo as an adult, in order to block out the harsher memories of the *real* school years: the homework, the halitosis and the heartbreak. Nobody wants to feel that they were not part of this culture, these memories, this collective unconscious, and so we allow history to be rewritten with our consent.

Naturally, we should do all we can to encourage our children to enjoy a wide range of play, including playing outside whenever it's possible or convenient. But we do ourselves a disservice if we let the memory cheat.

Chapter 23

Money's Too Tight to Mention

A survey commissioned by *Pregnancy & Birth* magazine in 2005 revealed that the average cost of bringing up a child from birth to age five was *£52,605*.

O f course, such surveys are misleading in both directions, as they presume the equipment will be bought new and do not take account of any attendant 'hidden costs'. These might be things like the need/desire to move to a bigger house (or one with a better garden or in a nicer area), or the loss of earnings through changing to part-time work. Or all those herbal teas you will be drinking in a dark room at the end of a stressful day. Or the extra trips to the pub to get away from the endless well-intentioned advice. Or the additional telephone bill from all the time spent on the phone moaning about the kids. And don't forget the costs of browsing the Internet just to depress yourself with statistics about how 'un-average' your child is.

If you take the time to read such surveys, you'll probably come away with the idea that you've been paying for a share of someone else's childcare and organic baby food while they've been subsidizing your baby bath and nappy cream – or the other way round.

Dedicated follower of fashion

Children are small. Therefore, you might reasonably expect their shoes to be a fraction of the price of your own. And so, venturing into a shop to buy some sole protection for your crawler, you can be forgiven for doing a double take when you first look at the price tag. There must be some mistake, you think. Has your infant suddenly turned into a *Sex And The City* devotee and begun demanding Manolos? Did the manufacture of two small pieces of leather footwear necessitate the slaughter of the last two members of an endangered species of lemur, or are the buckles made of some highly precious metal?

And then there's the clothes. Tiny things, you think, and they will cost maybe a quarter of what you might pay for a new jumper. Oh, no. It doesn't work like that. Mark-ups on children's clothes are enough to put such fripperies as caviar and South African gold in the shade. The first time you go into a normal high-street store and look at, say, a small woollen cardigan for a six-month-old, you'll take a step back and wonder if they have got the decimal point in the wrong place.

The children's clothes industry is a particularly mad one. You may well look at photos from twenty or thirty years ago and reflect that the sort of thing you were expected to wear as an infant was remarkably unpretentious – one might even say uncool. And do you know what? You weren't bothered. That yellow balaclava and pea-green cardigan knitted by Auntie Gladys were actually very practical, and there was nothing wrong with those sturdy hand-me-down purple corduroy dungarees – they were durable and good for getting covered in mud. But as with food, some-one decided a few years ago that children's clothing needed to be given something of a makeover. And suddenly, catalogues for children were springing up everywhere. Mums and dads were brainwashed into thinking that their children had to have apparel which was not just practical but stylish too. Well, okay, mainly mums. Because, if you're honest, it won't be you choos-ing your children's clothes very much, will it?

In fact, *86%* of parents with toddlers now spend more on their children's clothes than on their own. This will come as no surprise; you may wonder, actually, how 14% manage to do it the other way round.

This state of affairs will continue until they get to the age of about 32, when they decide that fashion is no longer worth bothering with and realize that, all this time, Marks & Spencer have been doing a range of really comfortable cardigans and stretch-waist trousers. Of course, by then, they will probably have small fashion victims of their own to spoil with the Jojo Maman Bébé catalogue to hand.

A bargain of necessity

The thing is, a lot of the stuff you 'need' just isn't necessary, and a lot of the time it is not even useful. Here are a few of the things which, in our own experience and in my own totally unscientific straw poll of other parents, were found to be *most useless* – in the hope that you'll benefit from other people's mistakes.

✗ *Expensive changing stations*, especially those in tasteful beech or pine. Just use a table.

✗ *Automatic nappy disposal gizmos*. Just bag the festering objects and bin them, please.

✗ *Electronic toys, e.g. exercisers*. Those which flash and make lots of noise are too distracting for children under four months, but fine for older babies and toddlers. Something to put away until the time is right.

✗ *Baby walkers*. Stories of accidents abound, there's no evidence that they help children to walk any earlier and they can get their entertainment in other ways. (Some cited them as useful, though. So I suppose the message here is to beg, borrow or steal them rather than buy them new.)

✗ *Lots of soft toys*. They just collect dust and babies don't hug them properly and derive comfort from them until they're older. You'd have to be hard-hearted to deprive your child of teddies, though, and people will inevitably give you lots of them as presents, so put them on a shelf until they are needed.

✗ *An electronic baby monitor*. Unless you live in a huge mansion, they will shout loud enough, don't worry. On the other hand, there are those who sing their praises – not for listening to Baby, but for eavesdropping on the couple next door having a row.

✗ *Video monitors*. Come on, this is your child. He's not a juvenile offender. Yet.

✗ *Very small posh clothes*. You'd be surprised how quickly they'll grow out of these. No matter how cute they look, don't bother; they may only wear them once. With the stuff which says 'New baby' or '0–3 months', go for the simplest possible.

✗ *Bootees.* Aaah. Aren't they cuuuute? … Forget it. Get kicked off and lost in minutes.

✗ *Designer buggy.* I'm sorry, but if you waste money on one of these, you're just sad. Your child is not a trophy. And I don't care if you do live in Notting Hill and everyone else has got one.

✗ *'Sleep positioners'.* Er, hello? Newsflash? Babies don't lie still.

✗ *Cot bumper.* Doesn't appear to make any difference sleep-wise, apart from the fact that you'll be lying awake in fear of it falling on top of them (and you'll get up every five minutes to check that it hasn't).

✗ *Silver-plated egg and spoon.* I'm sure the people who gave this to my correspondent spent ages looking for an original present.

✗ *Baby-wipe warmer.* Apparently it just burns some of the wipes to a frazzle and leaves the others stone cold. They soon get used to the feel of wipes on their bottoms.

✗ *Baby bath thermometer.* Are you really unable to dip your elbow in the water and work out how warm it is?

✗ *Well-known educationally 'stimulating' mobile* with black-and-white symbols on pieces of glossy card. When it comes to mobiles, the rules are simple: (1) They are babies. (2) They like cute fluffy animals. (3) So give them cute fluffy animals.

✗ Some people also mentioned *baby bathtubs, bouncers* and *slings* – not because they were especially useless in themselves but because they only got to use them three or four times.

On the other hand ...
It's only fair to list some of the items cited as being among the *most useful*. Again, it's worth getting to know people who will lend you them.

✓ *Rocker chair.* We found with each child that we'd put them down in it about a dozen times a day.

✓ *Playmat* with dangly bits designed to keep them occupied and provoke gurgles of delight while you get on with other jobs.

✓ *Things to wipe stuff up with.* Muslin or similar, which you can also put over your shoulder to protect your shirt.

✓ *Teddies.* The above notwithstanding, they will be a great source of comfort to your little one. Non-furry types are always safest for small babies.

✓ *Microwave bottle sterilizer.* The sort you can put four bottles and accoutrements in at once. Can be left to work its magic while you get on with something else. Ping! Oh, it's done.

✓ *Lots of bibs, vests and tops.* Imagine how many of these your child will get through, and then double it.

✓ *Hat.* A well-made hat to keep the sun off their sensitive skin is a wise investment. Assuming they keep it on, of course. Bear in mind that a baseball cap will probably get them banned from certain well-known shopping centres.

✓ *Ball.* A soft, multi-coloured play ball can be a source of delight and fascination for a baby – and a proper football, when they are older, is probably the most versatile toy they will ever have.

✓ *Rattles* and other small, hand-held toys, especially on car journeys.

✓ *Booster seat.* Clips on to an ordinary chair – take it everywhere and you don't have to queue for a high chair.

✓ *Hand-held vacuum cleaner.* You will be hoovering up after every meal.

✓ *'Messy bag.'* Small, zip-up PVC or plastic bag, like a pencil case, for transporting anything too horrible to go elsewhere. (That half-eaten banana which he will want later, for example.)

✓ *Digital thermometer.* As another parent put it, 'useful when pointing out to a sceptical doctor that your child has had a temperature of 101 for the last three days.' The Thermoscan Digital Ear Thermometer comes recommended.

Manufacturers of items aimed at babies and toddlers are running a business like any other. Their products may be advertised with a perky little fluffy-haired person who looks a bit like your perky little fluffy-haired person, but that doesn't mean they are a cute and cuddly company.

They're trying to squeeze every last penny out of you like everyone else – and they know that you, as a new parent, are at your most uninformed, helpless and gullible. They use a combination of reassurance ('your baby will be safe with this') and scaremongering ('proven to reduce occurrence of nappy rash/cot death/infant illiteracy/child growing up to be a feckless layabout'). Exercise common sense and discretion – just as you would with any other consumer item.

Chapter 24

If You Tolerate This, Your Children Will Be Next

Women surveyed by *New Woman* magazine in 2005 who intended to give up work altogether after having a family: *25%*
Women surveyed by *New Woman* magazine in 2005 who intended to work full-time and put children in nursery: *11%*

What happens when your child is ill? Try this:

She struggles out of bed, saying, 'It's all right, I'll manage,' before getting herself dressed and dosing herself up with Calpol. She makes her own appointment with the doctor at a convenient time after work, and then staggers bravely off to school, nursery or childminder with her chin up and a boxful of tissues in her bag. She comes home looking a bit pale maybe, but really not much worse than usual. She takes her medicine, retires for an early night with a hot-water bottle and emerges the next morning, back on her feet and ready to face the world.

Well, no.

True, some bosses acknowledge that children sometimes get ill, that ill children need adult supervision and that a child who's ill needs Mum or Dad. There is, though, often the assumption that you will somehow 'sort it out' and be in for work as usual. People with children, the thinking goes, are not a special case. What if Rhona from Accounts needed the morning off to take her dog to the vet, or Jeff from Sales had to be late in because his ailing Venus flytrap needed tending to? So what if your child may have rubella or pneumonia? I'm sorry, but we need to have that essential purchasing meeting, or that vitally important Mergers and Acquisitions Strategy seminar.

How do you deal with this? Obviously you need to make your superiors aware of your situation and reiterate that you are getting the work done, regardless of your other commitments. If anybody wants to use your status as parent against you, then you should point out, politely but firmly, that your life outside the office/site/whatever does not affect your work, and ask to be judged on your performance alone. It is not unreasonable to expect a little flexibility – especially if you are prepared to give some back.

The invisible enemy

All right, so most of the time it won't be rubella or pneumonia. It'll probably be a two-day stomach bug or a cold (children's colds always seem thoroughly miserable, and can make them very pale and withdrawn).

Children's illnesses always seem much more spectacular than your own. Everything is magnified. They rarely announce that they are feeling a little off colour and go for a nice quiet lie down in a dark room. Oh no. It's usually an *Exorcist*-style projectile vomit followed by a screech of anguish, and you're off.

Unless medical intervention is required, you'll dispense hugs, water or Calpol as required, and before long everything will be back to normal. But they still need one of you. Having a child isn't a part-time hobby. And when they are ill, that just goes double. Children who are ill need parental love, care and supervision more than ever. And sometimes, that means one parent taking the day off work – usually, the one whose work can be most easily covered or rearranged.

It's worst if you're self-employed; it means you're set back a day and may lose a day's business, possibly even lose contracts or clients. But at least the decision is yours. If you work for an employer, you immediately feel guilty for even asking. It's like you're some sort of weird leper or alien being. 'Sorry? You need to be at *home*? In case your child vomits? Well, is he not old enough to hold the bowl himself? … I don't know … Have you got someone to deputize for your 11 a.m. meeting?'

It's funny how much work amounts to pushing bits of paper from one desk to another, or flipping bytes of information from one chip to another, or pushing objects from one place to another. It's hard to believe anyone or anything is so essential to the functioning of mankind that you can't miss a day here and there, or catch up when you come back, or have the work covered by someone else – or even do it from home, depending on the amount of supervision your child needs. (If your work can be done on the computer and emailed in, and all they have is a bit of flu or chickenpox, you can sometimes get away with tucking them up on the sofa in front of a nice video and getting on with it.)

Some people find that their contracts will allow them only *unpaid* leave to look after children. If this is your employer's attitude, you could always just lie. Ring in and tell them you've got a stomach bug or a migraine. Your untruth is less damnable than their attitude, frankly.

Anyway, you'll be owed some days off. You will probably already have put in unfeasible amounts of unpaid overtime just to fit in with your company's assumptions, so you might reasonably assume that you are entitled to something back once in a while.

Also, there's the Great Myth Of Work – the idea that people who spend the longest in the office are those who put in the most productivity. Think about the colleagues you know. Just because they get into the office at 7 a.m. and leave at 7 p.m., that doesn't mean they will have done 12 hours of work at the end of the day. How much of that time is spent shuttling between appointments, having lunch, having coffee or gossiping? How much of it is spent in smoking breaks, flirting, waiting for the photocopier to warm up, checking cricket/football scores or investigating other more dubious material on the Internet? People get up to all sorts at work. If your worst sin is to have the occasional sickie to look after your child, then you're a better employee than most.

Chapter 25
It's the End of the World
As We Know It
(And I Feel Fine)

Swedish men who took no parental leave before 'Daddy-Month' paternity leave was introduced in 1995: *54%*
Swedish men who took no parental leave after 'Daddy-Month' paternity leave was introduced in 1995: *18%*

Heigh-ho, heigh-ho …

orking parents, it seems, are here to stay. In our circle of roughly 20 couples with children, there are only four mothers who do not work at all, and I've no reason to believe that is untypical.

You may hear people virtuously declaiming that a strong belief in mothers staying at home with children has determined that they should give up work. Forgive me for scenting the whiff of bovine excrement. Surely the key factor is the *ability* to give up work – mainly dictated by finances – rather than the principle of wanting to do so. You can have all the principles in the world, but if your mortgage was obtained on two salaries, the chances are that you'll need two salaries (or at least one and a half) to maintain it. You can believe all you want in the ideal of the stay-at-home mum, but most families have to pay the bills. Such things are hardly extravagant luxuries maintained by a disposable second income.

Received wisdom will tell you that any mother who goes out to work is a neglectful slattern, and moreover is heading for a burnout and a nervous breakdown and will have a delinquent for a child. Even your own older relatives may well express disapproval. This may not actually be phrased in critical terms as such; you may find leading questions being asked, such as, 'Does she really *need* to work, then, dear?' or, 'If you gave up the car/washing machine/weekly takeaway you could make some cutbacks …'

This is not the 1950s, and mothers who work are a perfectly normal and necessary part of life for most couples. How you and your lady structure the work–life balance will be up to you, and will depend on a number of factors such as:

- Your income.
- Your work situation.
- Your monthly outgoings.
- How well your child plays with others.
- Nursery/childminder provision in your area.

It's also good if employers realize that children can occasionally be ill, another aspect of everyday life which seems to pass many of them by (see Chapter 24).

Stop me if you've heard this one before

'A woman knows all about her children. She knows about dentist's appointments and romances, about best friends, about favourite foods, secret fears and hopes and dreams. A man is vaguely aware of some short people living in the house.' (Anon)

What is funny (peculiar) is how jokes like the anonymous one above seem to validate laughing at men in this way, while political correctness clamps its ugly jaws on anyone who dares to make a joke about the female of the species.

The media often chooses to highlight the imbalance whereby women take most of the childcare and are more likely to have time off work when children are ill. This is all well and good. But often the media can contribute towards these same assumptions.

In March 2005, BBC Radio 4's Woman's Hour featured a phone-in about mums who work: how they fit their hours around collecting children from school, how they have to be off work with ill children, and how their experience contrasts with that of the 'child-free' women who sometimes feel put upon and required to take second place when it comes to booking their leave. It was an interesting and valid discussion. It was a shame, though, that presenter Jenni Murray couldn't resist a comment about how 'disappointed' she was that so few men had contributed to the debate. I'm taking a wild stab in the dark here, but could that possibly be anything to do with the fact that the show is (a) called *Woman's Hour* and (b) on at 10 o'clock on a weekday morning? How many men, unless they work from home like me or are the main carer, would have been in a position to hear the programme broadcast live?

Even the *Guardian*, which one would expect to be more progressive than most, ran an entire two-page spread in February 2005 in its 'Parenting' section, assessing the old question of the 'working parent'. Eight mothers were featured – probably friends of the journalist, as this is the way these things are usually done – and *not one father*. One of the mums specifically mentioned she was a single parent, which is fair enough; otherwise, only one of the mini-interviews even mentioned Dad fitting the children in around his work commitments.

The idea that a man might make sacrifices for his children too is still a fairly revolutionary one – and yet thousands, *millions* of dads do so every day. If you do read an article about fathers being full-time or part-time carers, it's usually, even these days, written in a ho-ho, nudge-nudge, don't-you-feel-emasculated, let's-laugh-at-the-New-Men-and-I-bet-they-eat-lentils sort of way. And adverts for supermarkets, nappies, etc. always mention the 'best deals for Mum'. The presumption is always that only the mother has to adapt her life to children; Dad, if he is pictured at all, is still seen as the natural provider, not the natural parent. He needs to be taught how to spend time with his children. He's treated, in fact, rather like a child himself. No wonder we sometimes behave like them.

You'll find, unfortunately, that this is how things are often seen. Women are either (a) Selfless Earth-mothers who give everything up for their children or (b) Bad Women who go back to work and screw their kids up for life. Men, meanwhile, are hapless idiots who are there for the sex, pat the bump affectionately every couple of weeks for nine months, then disappear to the golf course. Oh, and we don't know how to do housework, either. Have you noticed? Those bumbling men in adverts who try to – wait for it, I can hardly contain myself – read the instructions on a packet of soap powder and – nurse, my sides – end up *pouring it all over the floor*! Laugh? I almost cried.

Man, I feel like a woman

More and more of us are taking on a proportion of the childcare, and recent moves to allow some of the extended maternity leave to be transferred to men must surely be welcomed. Taking equal responsibility, after all, is not exactly something you can do unless you are given equal support. Until recently, most men got a couple of days' paternity leave if they were lucky – and that was only after signing in blood to promise that, on going back, they would catch up on the in-tray, lick the boss's boots clean and work endless unpaid overtime.

It's still seen as odd for a man to ask for flexible working hours for childcare purposes. Men still have very little choice in the matter – it's work or die. And if you want to enter a female-dominated profession like primary-school teaching, childcare or some parts of the voluntary sector, attitudes are so entrenched that you might as well have *weirdo* emblazoned on your forehead.

So, once again, men are given a good kicking; we're forced back into traditional hunter-gatherer roles in order to support the family, and then bashed for not spending enough time with the children. You can't win. If you work all the hours God sends to ensure you keep your job and bring home the bacon (or tofu), then you are a heartless so-and-so who is married to the job and never gets to see his kids. On the other hand, if you make compromises at work in order to spend more time at home, then you're a feckless layabout who doesn't provide sufficiently for his family, and you're quite possibly a Beta Male.

Catch-22? Too right.

Father's day

You may go even further down this route and decide that you'll be the one doing the bulk of the care. There are a number of scenarios in which this surely makes sense, e.g. if your partner earns substantially more, or if she would really find it difficult to pick up her career after a break, or if you have some work that can be done outside the hours when the baby is awake.

Working in the evening and the small hours after caring for a child all day is not recommended, though. I tried this combination – well, for two days a week, anyway – and it was no fun. It's basically like doing double shifts with no sleep. I got a book out of it, but it drove me crazy.

An increasing number of fathers opt to be the stay-at-home carer and it's fascinating to read and hear of their experiences. The recurring theme seems to be the lack of a readily identifiable social circle for dads and their children. Toddler groups are aimed at mothers, and many of them are still called 'Mums & Toddlers' groups (often with apostrophes uncertainly bouncing around somewhere). Daytime events in libraries and community centres presume that Mum will be the one coming along. And so on, and so on. It's still hard, as a man, to break into a social circle composed entirely of women; you'll inevitably be regarded with hostility, suspicion or even pity. Even in liberal quarters, a man walking into a toddler group with his small child will cause a few double takes. 'What's he doing here?' they'll

be thinking. 'Why isn't he sweating in some grey cubicle somewhere deep in the city, earning a substantial bonus to keep his
wife in designer dresses?'

Anyway, I recommend a look at **www.homedad.org.uk**, a
fascinating site where some dads who have gone down this
route give their real-life stories. It's very eye-opening, and probably much more informative than any more of my sardonic
carping could ever be.

Chapter 26
Say Hello, Wave Goodbye

People agreeing that a government subsidy should be offered to grandparents involved in regular childcare: *64%*

ome time or another, you'll hear a plaintive wail from underneath the duvet of 'I don't want to *go* today,' and the subsequent conversation will pan out something like this:

'Well, what do you think you're going to do instead, Rebecca?'
'Stay in bed.'
'You can't stay in bed.'
'I want to.'
'Well … *why* don't you want to go?'
'Because it's boring.'
'Well, everyone has to do boring things, you know.'
'And they all hate me.'
'I'm sure that's not true, Rebecca.'
'Well, it is.'
'What am I going to tell them?'
'Say I'm ill.'
'I can't lie for you, darling. What are you going to do if you stay at home all day?'
'Watch telly.'
'Well … what are you going to eat if you stay at home?'
'Biscuits.'

'We haven't got any.'

'I'll just eat nothing, then.'

'Look, this is silly, Rebecca, you've *got* to go.'

'Why?'

'Because you're International Strategy Manager for a major consultancy firm, darling. And if you don't go to work we can't pay the mortgage this month.'

[Sigh.]

'Ooo-*kaaaaaay*. You get the kids up.'

The slippery nursery slopes

Yes, it's that fun time when you realize that, if you're going to keep a roof over your heads, you've both got to work for at least part of the week – and that, unfortunately, means finding some-one to look after the children.

You may be fortunate enough to have family nearby to call upon, but in these days of increasing geographical mobility, that may not be the case. The lobby group Grandparents Plus tells us that 5 million of the 13 million grandparents in the UK spend up to three days a week caring for their grandchildren, while a recent study has shown that up to 70% of parents use 'informal networks' (including their own parents) for childcare.

However, grandma and grandad aren't necessarily going to want to spend all their free time looking after the children. They want a life too – they want to take advantage of the 'leisure society' suddenly offered to the over-50s, and the chances are that they'd rather be out abseiling, paragliding and marathon running. Sadly, they'll probably have a better social life than you do. So, unless one of you works for one of those progressive (and wealthy) companies that provide a built-in crèche, you're going to have to do a bit of shopping around.

There is a lot in the media about the supposedly detrimental effects on children of childminders and nurseries. It's not that there's any more than there ever was, it's just that when you have children aged between, say, one and four, you suddenly find yourself tuned into this stuff – like short-wave bleeps and burbles resolving itself into coherent speech, it's just suddenly *there*. Everyone has an opinion, and more often than not it's a parent-bashing one – designed, as ever, to make you feel guilty about the choices you have to take. You could read a particularly persuasive article and come away with the idea that, if you send your children to a pre-school nursery, they'll turn into the most appalling illiterate delinquents who will hate you for the rest of your life. It's best just to tune this sort of thing out. Just imagine if this person were saying these things to you face-to-face. 'Sorry,' you'd reply, 'I can't hear what you're saying over the sound of your axe being ground.'

All children are different. You should both take a business-like approach, tempered with a soft heart, and decide between you what's best for your children. Some children will thrive in the sociable atmosphere of a nursery, others will enjoy the quieter environment offered by a childminder, while others may be happiest mixing and matching. Some will respond best to the continuity of the same environment every day, while others will be bored by this and may be more stimulated by having, say, a childminder on Monday, grandma on Tuesday, nursery two or three days a week, etc. Of course, you may not have a choice, but if the decision is there to be made, don't let anyone else make it for you.

Never mind old-fashioned values – the most scandalous aspect of childcare is the fact that it is so horrendously expensive. You may find a childminder who charges by the hour and only for the hours she actually works. If so, you're very lucky indeed. You'll usually have to pay during the school holidays as well if you want to keep them, which in many cases will mean that they have a better holiday-pay deal than you'd ever have. Can you think of any other self-employed people who enjoy a paid holiday?

Lay down some rules, though. If you're paying for their services it's not unreasonable that you expect them to be on call. You'll have none of this disappearing to Florida for two weeks on full pay because 'you were off anyway' (the ultimate in cheek, if you ask me). Meanwhile, nurseries whose fees err on the side of reasonable are rarer than rocking-horse droppings. You may start to wonder if work–life balance exists – or if it is just available as a sort of contractual obligation, and deliberately made it out of many people's financial reach. In the UK, when your child reaches the age of three, you are entitled to 'nursery vouchers' from the government, but these only subsidize a certain number of sessions. It may seem obvious, but if subsidized sessions run from 1 p.m. to 3 p.m. and whichever of you is doing the transport run can't get away from work until 4.30 p.m. at the earliest … do, as they say, the maths.

If you both intend to work, it will be almost impossible for your child to attend a school nursery with this arrangement of hours, so you need to explore other options. For private nurseries, remember that the cheapest won't be the best – visit several, and take a good look around. Are the children happy, and active? Do they have plenty to keep them occupied? Is there a good staff–child ratio? Ask to see a plan, an inspectors' report, and some examples of things children have produced (paintings, models, photos, etc.). How does the place *feel*? Often there will be something you just can't put into words.

Picture this
On the plus side, children who go to nursery often learn more quickly to play with their peers and to pick up new skills. And

you will be amazed by the things they bring home. It's only when they start to indulge in art and craft activities away from home that you get enough objectivity to realize how truly rubbish most children's efforts in this department really are.

Yes, of course, they are made by your little darlings' own sweet hands, so your heart will be telling you that you have a budding Rodin or Monet (or Tracey Emin) on your hands. Your head, though, will be telling you otherwise.

Sometimes you won't even be sure which way up the pictures are supposed to go. At other times, you will wonder why your child has chosen one colour to become fixated upon. You may even contemplate ringing up the nursery to ask them if there are, in fact, any other colours of paint available on Jessica's table, as she appears to have rendered all sixteen of her last masterpieces in what you can only describe as Varicose Vein Blue.

The models are a joy to behold, as well. You'll lose count of the number of shakers (made of a toilet roll covered in coloured paper and filled with rice) which you will acquire, not to mention the innumerable spaceships, houses, cars, garages and shops, all of which are, essentially, a cereal box with milk-bottle-tops, coloured paper and various spangly bits stuck all over them. As you take the thing out of the bag, with glitter and sequins dropping all over the carpet, you have to try really hard not to pull a face and say something like, 'Couldn't you at least have painted it?'

Faced with your very own growing cardboard city on top of the kitchen cupboards or under the table, you will have to steam in there like a particularly heartless politician – tough on clutter, tough on the causes of clutter – and smuggle the lot of them into the dustbin when Toddler is occupied. While he is filling his face with chocolate is usually a good time. If he asks about it, just feign ignorance.

There is a big plus side. Don't worry if your infant is producing piles of junk, with no attempt to make them aesthetically pleasing or imbued with any kind of meaning. Fear not if he does paintings which are basically just misshapen splodges, whose total ineptitude leaves you wondering whether he has the hand–eye co-ordination of the average orangutan. Based on this, he will probably have a great future exhibiting in the Saatchi Gallery in twenty years' time. (See below.)

Interlude: Gallery

'Abstract' by E. Blythe, aged 4 ¾ . Or, in fact, a masterpiece of modern art?

The *Guardian* newspaper displayed a sense-of-humour failure when I sent in some toddler scribbles and suggested they might like to display them on the cover of *G2* along with the other contemporary art which they had featured. I should perhaps have pointed out that it is medically dangerous to be *quite* so far up your own backside.

Chapter 27

Wonderful Life

precocious *adj*. often *derog*. (of a person, esp. a child) prematurely developed in some faculty or characteristic.

 ere are some examples of *interesting character traits or skills* which your child may exhibit or develop.

Rhetoric

A little boy was talking to his teacher about whales. The teacher said it was physically impossible for a whale to swallow a human because, even though it was a very large mammal, its throat was very small. The little boy put his hand up and stated that Jonah was swallowed by a whale. Irritated, the teacher reiterated that a whale could not swallow a human; it was physically impossible. The little boy said, 'When I get to heaven I'll ask Jonah, then.' The teacher asked, 'What if Jonah went to hell?' The little boy replied, 'Well, then you can ask him.'

Honesty

At an Easter morning church service, the children were invited to come forward. One little girl was wearing a particularly pretty dress and, as she sat down, the vicar leaned over and said, 'That's very pretty. Is it your Easter dress?' The little girl replied, 'Yes, and Mummy says it's a bugger to iron.'

More Honesty

Four-year-old James came running out of the bathroom, shouting to his dad that he'd dropped his toothbrush in the toilet. 'It's all right,' said Dad, 'I'm sure it was an accident. We'll just throw it away.' So Dad retrieved the toothbrush and threw it in the rubbish bin. James stood for a moment thinking hard, then ran back to the bathroom and came back with Dad's toothbrush. He smiled and held it up. 'Daddy, shall we throw this one away as well? Because it fell in the toilet last week.'

Logic
A nursery school teacher was reading the story of The Three Little Pigs. She came to the part where the first pig approaches the man who has a bundle of wood and the pig says, 'Please, Mister, may I have some wood to build a house?' Looking around, the teacher asked, 'And what do you think the man said?' One little girl's hand went up. 'Yes, Daisy?' said the teacher. 'Please, Miss,' said Daisy, 'I think he probably said, "Blimey! A talking pig!".'

Incisiveness
When a woman friend of mine was eight months pregnant, her three-year-old daughter came into the bathroom and said: 'Mummy, you're reeeeally fat!' Keeping her cool, the mother replied, 'Yes, darling. Mummy has a baby growing in her tummy, you remember?' The girl answered, 'I know *that*, Mummy. So what's that growing in your bottom?'

Literal thinking
Phone salesman: 'Hello, could I speak to your mum, please?'
Boy: 'She's asleep.'
Salesman: 'All right, your dad then?'
Boy: 'He's at work.'
Salesman: 'Well, is there anyone else there I could speak to?'

Boy: 'My sister.'
Salesman: 'OK, please may I speak to your sister?'
Boy: 'Wait a minute.'
[Very long silence on the phone.]
Boy: 'Hello?'
Salesman: 'Oh, I thought you were going to call your sister?'
Boy: 'I did. But I can't get her out of her cot.'

Lateral thinking

A small boy is sent to bed by his father. Five minutes later:

'Da-ad-yyy…'
'What?'
'I'm thirsty. Can I have a drink of water?'
'No. You had your chance. Lights out.'

Five minutes later:

'Da-aaaad-yyyyyy!'
'WHAT?'
'I'm *thir*-sty! Can I have a drink of waaaaa-ter?'
'I said no. If you ask again, I'm going to come in and be very cross.'

Five minutes later:

'*Daaaa-aaaadyyyyy!! …*'
'WHAT is it now??!'
'When you come in to be very cross, can you bring me a drink of water?'

Deduction
Little Gemma was sitting and watching her dad and she suddenly noticed that he had several strands of grey hair. She looked at her father and asked, 'Daddy, why are some of your hairs grey?' Her dad replied, 'Well, it's like this. Every time that you do something wrong and upset me or make me unhappy, one of my hairs turns grey.' Gemma pondered this revelation and then said, 'So, daddy – is that why *all* of Grandma's hairs are grey?'

Natural justice
A paramedic responded to a call from a woman in labour, and when he got to the house he found there had been a power cut. As the house was so dark, the paramedic asked three-year-old Lucy to hold a torch high over her mummy so he could see while he helped deliver the baby. Lucy diligently did as she was asked. Her mum pushed and pushed and, after a while, Lucy's little brother was born. The paramedic lifted him by his little feet and, in time-honoured fashion, spanked him on his bottom. The boy began to cry. The paramedic then thanked the wide-eyed Lucy for her help and asked her what she thought about what she had just witnessed. Lucy's quick answer was, 'He shouldn't have crawled in there in the first place.'

Foresight
The children had all been photographed, and their teacher was now trying to get them each to buy a copy of the group photo. They weren't keen, and she had to try a bit of persuasion. 'Just think how nice it will be to look at it when you are all grown up,' she said. 'You'll be able to look at the photo and say, "There's Jennifer, she's a lawyer", or, "That's Michael, he's a doctor".'

And a small boy at the back of the room called out, 'And there's the teacher. She's dead.'

Innocence

A mother was trying hard to get some obstinate tomato ketchup out of a bottle for four-year-old Tom's fish fingers, and she had resorted to the time-honoured technique of banging the container hard on the underside. During her struggle the phone rang, so she asked Tom to answer it. 'It's the vicar, Mum,' said Tom to his mother. Then he added, 'Sorry, Mummy can't come to the phone. She's hitting the bottle.'

Chapter 28
There She Goes

Parents who say their child 'regularly' hits other children: *44%*
EU member states which have a law against smacking: *9*

Hit me baby one more time

People will quite readily tell you how little sleep you're going to get, and how you're never going to have a sex life again as long as you live. They will gleefully impart to you that your house will reek of mashed turnip, disinfectant and faeces. They will take great delight in explaining to you that, as a dad, your role is basically to walk into the chemist, the supermarket and the clothes shop, hand over your debit and credit cards and tell them to take whatever they need. But the one thing nobody ever seems to tell you is how *violent* your kids can be.

We're not talking about teenagers thumping each other in the playground, or glassy-eyed eight-year-olds whacked up on tartrazine and Cheerios, zapping aliens on a PlayStation screen until three in the morning and slumping exhausted under the table at school the next day. Although these things happen, obviously. No, we're talking, as ever, about babies and toddlers. Here are just a few of the ways they can inflict serious injury on a parent:

- *Head-butting while getting them dressed.* Small toddlers, with their frog-like legs, are adept at this one. Don't let their head get under your chin, whatever you do. Because one moment you'll be pulling his trousers up, and the next he'll have straightened his legs, and his small, bullet-like cranium will whack you with a rabbit-punch.
- *Flailing arms and legs.* Especially dangerous if they have climbed into bed between you. Toddlers are not great respecters of other people's space, as you will have noticed when watching them play.
- *Armed and dangerous.* Do you know how hard the surface of a child's plastic or wooden toy is? You soon will.
- *Chaaaaaaarge!* Small children love to run full tilt around houses and especially enjoy running into your arms from a great dis-

tance. This can be fun, but if they get enough momentum – and believe me, they sometimes do – it can be enough to bowl you over. Console yourself with the thought that your child may have a great future in rugby or American football.

Top five annoying toddler habits

Some things seem universal, and it's not hard to pull together a hit parade of the most irritating things which small children plague you with.

5 *The variable speed button*

They trudge along when you want them to hurry up, as if stepping in thick mud, and end up being dragged along at a 45-degree angle. On the other hand, they scamper about like tiny dynamos when you want them to slow down. It's the law.

4 *The lack of empathy*

Toddler's perception of relationships within the universe:

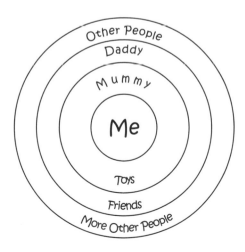

3   *Never being satisfied*
'But why, Daddy, why?'

2   *The mess/destruction*
As described in Chapter 30.

1   *The whingeing*
It's turned on at the slightest provocation. There is a particular, insidious tone of voice which all toddlers seem to have picked up by the time they are three or four, and if this is not addressed it will escalate in a matter of minutes into full-scale tears and screaming. But you can't give them everything they want all the time, and they need to learn that. It's not surprising that journalist Julie Burchill wrote about observing families on holiday with 'the children like little jailers, demanding everything.'

I'd like to see some vocal non-parents get a dose of reality in the form of a few days looking after a pair of hyperactive toddlers. There's a Reality TV series in it, I'm sure – *Parent For A Week*, or something. It's probably being commissioned as I write.

Chapter 29
Blue Monday

'It's pathetic when people just swear for the sake of it,' said former Sex Pistol Glen Matlock in a 2005 radio interview.[1]

One of the things it was probably hardest to understand yourself as a child was how on earth your parents could one minute be yelling their heads off in red-faced anger, and the next be laughing away as if nothing had happened. Surely they were angry? Surely they were in a bad mood, and therefore unlikely to find anything funny? How could we go back to normal after that wall-shaking bellow?

Language, Timothy

At the age of three, my daughter ran up to me and informed me in portentous tones that the electricians we'd had in for the afternoon had 'eaten all of Mummy's bloody chocolate!'

This kind of thing is quite amusing at first – it even has a kind of incongruous cuteness, as the child of that age cannot possibly be using the words in a deliberately offensive way. The one thing child experts agree on, though, is that you mustn't explode with anger if your little darling appears to have become a miniature Tarantino. For a small child, there's no level of difference between the word 'shit' and the word 'banana' – they are both new words which they have learned by hearing them and are keen to try out.

Obviously, though, they need to be made aware that there are certain words which are only appropriate for adults, and even then only in particular circumstances. Your child will probably develop

---

1   Of course, if you repeat this to anybody under the age of 20, they will look at you blankly and wonder what on earth a Sex Pistol is. Just say they were like Eminem.

an intuitive sense of when it's not appropriate to swear. You will have to become the most clean-mouthed, virtuous citizen you have ever known, unless you want your youngster to be seen as the local equivalent of MC MuthaF***a and Da Urban Posse.

The good dad's guide to swearing

- Save your invective for nights away from the little ones. It may be mildly funny the first time round when your three-year-old refers to a local dignitary as a 'git'. But the amusement is somewhat diluted when she goes up to Auntie Doris, bright-eyed and eager, and asks her what a 'bloody bastard' is.
- Be a model of restraint – houses up and down the land are full of weekend-DIY-expert fathers trying to put up shelves, accidentally hitting their thumbnails with hammers and loudly proclaiming, 'Oh, my goodness me! That jolly well hurt, I can tell you!'
- Invent harmless equivalents – it won't take long to adjust to saying 'Sugar!' when you spill some milk, or 'Fudge!' when you miss a bus. The word 'bollards' gained common currency in our household for a while. This worked well until the council installed a traffic-calming system on the nearby main road which actually involved some bollards, and we found it impossible to refer to them without Big Girl gasping, raising her eyebrows and proclaiming that we had said a Naughty Word.
- Maybe this goes without saying, but it's probably best to wait a while before showing them any *South Park* videos.

Sticks and stones

Your child will probably start hearing some colourful language when he/she starts school, if not before. Things have changed, though. You will probably remember a Child Who Swore in your own class at school, and the resulting moment of shock and outrage which finally resulted in this pupil being suspended, or at the very least given a serious punishment.

These days, primary school pupils think nothing of tossing fornicatory and defecatory expletives in the direction of the head's office before kicking their way outside for a game of knife-throwing, after which they'll go round the back of the bins for a quick drug transaction.

Okay, it hasn't got *that* bad, but in these liberal times swearing, for some reason, is no longer seen as a huge mark of disrespect, nor is it punished accordingly. All you can do is uphold your standards in your own home, and hope you get a head teacher who is on the same wavelength. Obviously you will not be able to shield your child from swearing altogether. There will be moments, such as when your car has a near-miss, or you drop the entire contents of a plate on the kitchen floor, or you burn your finger on the cooker … we've all done it. You can tackle the issue head-on if you like, by telling your child that there are certain circumstances when Mummies and Daddies say certain words, but you don't expect to hear them from children.

So when the vicar's over for tea (does that ever happen except in amusing situations contrived for humorous potential?) you can expect your offspring to come up to you and ask, 'Dad, I knocked my bricks over – is it OK to say "fuck"?'

Interlude: A small point

When your child says 'I need the toilet', she doesn't mean in ten minutes, or in five minutes, or even in one minute.
She means *now*.
So find one. Quick.
And remember where it is for next time.

Chapter 30
People Get Real

A 2005 survey tells us that parents spend £172,000,000 a year repairing the damage to their houses caused by toddlers.[1]

---

1   Emotional wreckage not included.

Every so often, there seems to be a feature in a weekend colour supplement about an ethereal-looking Scandinavian designer – often called Astrid and usually with fantastic bone structure – who has managed to combine 'family living' with 'urban minimalism'. Her luminous house has pale, stripped pine floors and trendy-looking leather storage chests and she has her books all ranged in order of size on cube-shaped shelves. There's nothing on the table but a leaf-shaped bowl containing a handful of blue pebbles. She is usually pictured posing against a sunlit doorway, smiling wistfully; in front of her can be seen time-delay images of her two blond children, Magnus and Ivo, scurrying around in the foreground. The boys are playing with wooden trains on the clean, smooth surface of the floor.

You find yourself imagining that, after the photographer had gone, Astrid breathed a sigh of relief, lit a fag and changed into a shell-suit. Meanwhile, Magnus whacked Ivo round the head with his train and started scribbling on the wooden floor with indelible marker pen, before upending a stack of books and trampling on them.

Yes, you too may have had aspirations to minimalism. But it's not really compatible with stacks of play dough, squeaky plastic things and noisy electronic gizmos. The best you can hope for is some kind of chest or set of storage boxes or similar, into which you can dump everything after bath time so that you don't have to look at it.

The mess is horrendous. Toddlers and pre-schoolers don't tidy up after themselves. Most suburban living rooms where toddlers play will contain some or all of the following:

• Cushion, smeared with brown substance of unknown origin. Best not to pay close attention.

- Strange mark on wall, again of unknown origin. May possibly approximate to size and shape of toddler hand.
- Several toy cars, located beneath sofa and scattered across floor.
- Jigsaw pieces, ditto.
- Doll, lying prone and sometimes frighteningly headless.
- Videos/DVDs, helpfully extracted from boxes and arranged in random pattern across carpet.
- Odd beeping noises, which will make you think the smoke alarm needs its batteries replacing – until you find the Interactive Thomas the Tank Engine secreted behind the armchair.
- Instructions for electronic toy you're not even sure you have any more, and which you would have killed to find three months ago when they were screaming at you to get it to work.
- Half-chewed breadstick.

They may, at the end of the day, be cajoled into helping put things into boxes, as part of the 'game', but it's an attraction which soon palls. And the last thing they're going to do is put one toy away before getting another one out. Locating broken or lost pieces is not top of their priority list, either. If you suggest they should round up the bits which have slid under sofas and behind cushions, they give you a look which says, 'Why should I do that? It's more than my job's worth.'

The edge of destruction

It's amazing, really – when you have a small, active person you spend ages making the house safe for them with stairgates, fridge locks, anti-bump corners on tables and so on. And yet they still manage to get round these, cause devastation and bump themselves. Are they secretly trained for this?

If you have a baby or toddler, you will not escape – be prepared for everything from the minor (tomato stains on your carpet) to the major (actual damage to the structure of the house). Top toddler damage includes:

- Broken windows.
- Permanent marker stains on furnishings.
- Blocked pipes.
- Chipped paintwork on doors.
- Damaged electrics.
- Floods caused by turning on taps.

Careful with that stairgate, Eugene

And then there are accidents involving other household items. Basically, if it's not nailed down it will be in danger of being broken, believe me. You can move your vases out of reach, put the special cut-glass bowl that Aunt Gertrude gave you away in a cupboard and hide your souvenir tankard from the 1993 Munich Beer Festival somewhere in the attic – but there will always be something.

Our first proper 'incident' involved a stairgate in front of the kitchen – our house at the time was built on a hill, so the kitchen was a good foot or so lower than the dining room and so was accessed by a step. The stairgate, we thought, kept the kitchen suitably separated from the rest of the house. We hadn't banked, though, on Toddler's tenacity and strength. Despite being told repeatedly not to swing on the gate, she found it hugely entertaining to do so – until the day her weight pulled the whole thing out of its housing (stairgates come with remarkably inadequate wall-fixings which rely largely on pressure) and sent her and the gate crashing into the kitchen. No serious harm done – but she didn't forget that in a hurry.

Can you do anything to prevent this? Not really. The toddler is naturally untidy, unhygienic and destructive, and the best you can do is to try to contain the mess. If you have a bespoke play-room, then lucky you – shut the door and forget about it. For most people, though, the reality will be the toy car poking you between the buttocks when you settle down for the evening's TV, and the squelch that tells you that somebody has secreted their half-chewed banana beneath the sofa cushion again.

They like to leave traps for the unwary. It's a war of nerves, and a war of attrition. Only time will help you win it.

Perhaps when they finally leave home, you can look forward to returning to a life of Spartan minimalism again. Until they turn up at the door with a suitcase full of dirty washing.

Chapter 31
I Predict a Riot

Instructions on aspirin bottle:
'In case of headache, take twice daily. Keep away from children.'

You may think that the reason for holding children's parties is to celebrate an important milestone in your young one's life, while providing a safe and enjoyable environment in which they can let off steam.

No.

The reason for holding children's parties is to remind yourself that there are, in fact, children out there who are even more badly behaved than your own.

Everyone will find the kind of party that suits them. But unless you are a very, very laid-back person indeed (or on soft drugs) you will become a frazzled, nervous wreck at the sight of what fifteen screaming infants whacked up on pink cake are doing to your soft furnishings. And when you next come to play your favourite album, you'll find someone has mysteriously removed it and replaced it with a CD of nursery rhymes. So, if you can possibly help it, don't have the party in your house.

That's entertainment

If you're going to hire a professional entertainer, it really is worth getting the best one you can afford. Don't run the risk of going budget and finding you've hired a miserable so-and-so who hates kids and just twists balloons for forty minutes. There are some genuinely innovative children's entertainers out there, hardy and vibrant souls who can command the attention of a roomful of three- and four-year-olds with a combination of magic, music and mirth. They are worth every penny. Get one in good time. Otherwise you'll be making those balloon rabbits yourself, and your audience will eat you alive.

Do ask your children what they want. My own Darling Daughter, at the age of four, declaimed to the world that she 'hated discos', which we were luckily told in time. It's a comment I am saving up to remind her about in ten years' time when she is putting on the glitter and lipstick for Nineties Night down at the Roximetric, or whatever.

Games without tears
It's useful to have a few games up your sleeve, and many of them don't require all that much in the way of resources.

- *Hide-and-seek.* An old standby, and if you have disregarded the advice above and are having the party in your house, there will obviously be a good few places to hide. Make sure you clearly delineate any out-of-bounds places, though – you don't want any accidents on the cellar steps.
- *Musical statues.* Play the music, everyone dances. Stop the music, everyone stands still. Repeat until you are thoroughly sick of it. You should really eliminate anyone who moves until a winner is left. In practice, this will involve you pointing at children and saying, 'You moved!' while they laugh derisively and refuse to go and sit down. It's a great way to make yourself unpopular.
- *Musical bumps.* As above, only when you stop the music they have to thump heavily to the floor. Whatever you do, don't be persuaded to join in – you'll feel it in whichever part of you is currently suffering.
- *Pass the parcel.* Which, these days, is always fixed so that everyone gets to do a layer. The modern thinking on this seems to be that layers need to be interspersed with small packets of sweets or other such prizes. There will probably be a bright five-year-old in the circle who's done this before, and who will work out that, as first layer-opener, she won't be the one to get the present. You have to get up early to catch these kids out. As you'll know.

She bangs the drums
And just how much *children's music* can you take?

No, I'm not talking about Busted, McFly, Britney or any of the other nominal pop stars whose singles are predominantly downloaded by the under-10s. I'm talking about those CD compilations of 'well-loved' songs and rhymes sung by someone you have never heard of, usually to the accompaniment of a plinky-plonky keyboard, a folky guitar and/or a drum-machine, all with lots of echo chamber to make it sound as if it's been recorded in a dungeon. Children don't ask for this kind of stuff. Parents buy it for them because they think they will want it played to them. *We can stop the madness.* You are a modern dad – get a grip. Make your child a compilation of your favourite classics, rock songs or indie greats, and get it on early.

Chances are that your good lady won't be bothered about this. You'll recall a time when, oddly, she was into the same music as you, or when there was at least some overlap. Hanging on to your old CDs, vinyl and tapes is very much a male thing: you just can't imagine *High Fidelity* with a female protagonist, can you? The theory goes that mums, once they have been subjected to the noise of screaming babies, rather lose the appetite for playing Curve or The Pixies at full blast.[1]

Bags of fun
This little innovation will probably get you sounding off in good parental manner about 'what the world is coming to'. You know the kind of thing. In your day, children were grateful for what they got, everyone said 'please' and 'thank you', you went outside and played in puddles in all weathers and that never did you any harm, there wasn't all this 24-hour TV for kids and what

---

1 This argument doesn't really hold water, because you will have heard at least some of the screaming too ... won't you?

you watched was much better anyway, you didn't have all these computer games and you made your own entertainment with two pieces of bark, some string and a frisbee, you'd ride your bike out in the street until twilight and nobody would worry or think you were causing a nuisance, etc., etc. – and most of all, you didn't go to someone else's party expecting to come away with a *party bag*. At this point you stomp off, go and shut yourself in the bathroom in disgust, and glance in the mirror – only to realize you have finally turned into your parents.

It can be argued that party bags are a Really Bad Idea. However, not giving them out now will, unfortunately, make you appear mean. Don't go overboard with them, because you don't want to embarrass anyone – after all, it's generally thought bad form to bring a present to a party which costs less than the one you go away with. (Yes, this happened to us.)

Most of the time, the actual contents of the bag matter very little – it's just the act of handing one out. Usually it's enough to throw in:

a) slice of cake;
b) party-blower;
c) small toy or two;
d) some form of confectionery snack.

These will be, respectively:

a) half-eaten by child on the way home and/or shoved under the car seat;
b) blown loudly to annoy parents for a few days, before being binned;
c) broken and/or lost within 24 hours;
d) eaten immediately, smeared on clothes, or binned by parent disgusted at calorific/teeth-rotting content.

You can see why people don't bother spending an awful lot on them.

If you want to do 'alternative' party bags hand woven in hessian, containing sugar-free snacks, a pomegranate, a recycling leaflet, a carton of organic milk and a small collection of inspirational poetry, then that's up to you. I think you know what will probably happen to it.

The dad's guide to getting out of children's parties

- *Double-book.* Secretly find out the date and 'accidentally' arrange to be visiting your parents or other relatives that weekend. It's worthy – and hard to get out of.
- *Go to work.* Have something come up at very short notice. Make sure it is important and that only you can do it. If you have a colleague who can phone you on your mobile at a pre-arranged time, this is even better. If you work shifts, be working that day; or cover for someone who's ill.
- *Do some home improvement.* Find some tasks that need to be done: cutting the hedge, mowing the lawn, doing some washing, or fixing that door handle which has been bothering you for months.
- *Be ill.* Drinking too much the night before will ensure this, but will lose you a bit in the sympathy stakes. A mystery 'flu' is good, and even better is something children could contract – so you are staying at home in the best interests of other people's kids. Potential chickenpox is ideal for scaring people off, although this can backfire – some parents are only too keen for their little darlings to catch this so they can get it over and done with in the school/nursery holidays. Play it by ear.
- *Split the care.* If you have two children and the invitation is for the older one only, make sure you get to stay at home with the

younger one (or vice-versa). Arrange one of his favourite activities and make sure he knows that it will be *daddy* taking him.

And if you really can't get away:

* *Put yourself in charge* of something important, something which keeps you busy and may prevent you from having to take part in any games – sorting out the drinks is a good one, while running the music is another. The latter is a good way of making sure you get maximum quality and minimum 'Nellie The Elephant'.
* *Grit your teeth* and remember that this is for the children, not for you. Problem is, you may reach the point where children's parties, as they are ubiquitous, may be the only time you get to socialize with your friends – so the temptation to turn them into afternoon drinking sessions is sometimes irresistible. (You stand there with this vague recollection that you used to go to parties where the attendees were over three feet high – and perhaps not quite as messy and slightly less loud.)
* If the weather is good, *unleash them outside*. In fact, you can do this even if it's cold; nothing need deter you, short of torrential rain or heavy snow. If you have any accessible space at all, whether it is a small backyard or a medium-sized garden or a nearby park, decant the darlings there as soon as is humanly possible, and make yourself comfortable in the living room with a handful of adult guests. Occasionally send someone to stick their head out of the back door and make sure nobody has pushed anyone else into the flowerbed yet.

The ten worst things about hosting children's parties
1 You crack open a beer at about midday, confident that at least a few of the other dads will join you when they arrive

– and you find they are all driving and want to stick to the orange juice.

2 You have to buy sweets and fizzy drinks which your own kids wouldn't normally have, and then you find they get a taste for them.

3 They have to have party bags. Allegedly.

4 Someone takes off the CD of late-80s and early-90s alternative rock which you spent the previous night burning so as to Educate The Kids, and puts the *Tweenies' Greatest Hits* on instead.

5 You find yourself being used as a vaulting horse by every child present.

6 You need to sort out an altercation because someone is playing with a toy someone else wanted.

7 You can't even escape to the bathroom for five minutes' peace, because it is permanently occupied by defecating infants.

8 Every other adult there is as exhausted as you are, and it's a strain to hold an intelligent conversation.

9 Something will get broken. Just make sure it isn't you.

10 You will be picking crushed crisps out of the carpet for the next three weeks, not to mention quietly sobbing as you extricate slices of cake from the video, wipe down jelly-encrusted walls and scrape squashed chocolate buttons from the recesses of your sofa.

The best thing about children's parties
After two hours or so, everyone is usually bored and wanting to go home. And you're not going to stop them.

The lowdown
Children's parties are the price you pay for your child being happy and having friends. So grin and bear them.

Chapter 32
Zeroes and Ones

Men surveyed by YouGov for Mothercare who would like to be able to stay at home and look after children rather than go to work: *69%*

Experts recommend quite a few ways in which you can keep your child stimulated, interested and acquiring new information. Books are vital to a child's development and Chapter 33 goes into that side of things a bit more. It also may not surprise you that they pick up a lot of what they learn from the television – and we'll have a look at that in Chapter 34. But babies are able to see and hear from the moment they are born (you knew that, didn't you?) and children supposedly learn as much in the first four years of their lives as they do in the next thirteen. So you may like to consider these other ideas.

Activity narration
A running commentary on activities, so that your child picks up words and develops thinking. Also known as 'talking to yourself'. You'll be walking along like one of those people with a space-age mobile phone attachment in their ear, chattering away for the benefit of Toddler. 'Come on, Lucy, ooh, look at that moss on the wall. Yes, it's green, isn't it? Doesn't it look funny? And there goes a fire engine. Nee-nah, nee-nah. Okay, yes, it's more like *weeeeeeeeooohhhh*, isn't it? Well, they used to go nee-nah, nee-nah when I was little. Hmm, look, there's a blue car. Yes, bluuuueeee. We like blue, don't we? Well, maybe you prefer pink. I don't know.' And so on, and so on. Continue until exhausted, or sectioned, or bedtime finally arrives.

Foreign language cassettes and videos

If you want to be the ultimate pushy parent, you can bear in mind that children are meant to acquire non-native languages much more easily at pre-school age than later on, so now's the time to start them off. (But if they live in Yorkshire, they will naturally grow up bilingual anyway; nothing will match the joy of the middle-class parent who first hears their lisping four-year-old come out with 'Ey oop, mam, weeeerz me tea?')

Computer software for toddlers

Quite good fun for you as well, as you'll find that, unlike with any of the proper computer games on the market, you are actually able to negotiate these successfully. Even when stressed and sleep-deprived, you still ought to be able to help Bob The Builder get Lofty to lift the blocks into place and get a 'well done' from your virtual friend. It's a lot more satisfying than zapping aliens. Resist the temptation to say 'Of course, in my day, all we had was the Sinclair ZX-81 with a 16K RAM pack.' You may as well be talking about the steam engine. Your child will not have a clue what you are going on about, and will not care.

Alphabet letters for fridge, bathtub etc.

Just make sure you don't forget where you are and idly end up spelling out rude words. Inevitably, non-parent visitors will not be able to resist this.

Star charts

No, not the sort that give you the location of Orion's belt – we're talking about the big piece of paper on the kitchen wall, sporting a little galaxy of sticky stars achieved for helpfulness, politeness and not dunking little sister's head in the porridge. When they reach a certain number of stars, a prize of some sort is forthcoming. Opinion, of course, is divided as to whether such bribery is effective in maintaining good behaviour. Do the little darlings actually think through their behaviour and adjust it accordingly, or are they just after the rewards? You tell me.

Phonics toys and other electronic spelling aids
Amusingly, most of these are pre-programmed to prevent you from producing four-letter words. Some of those development meetings must have been fun when they were deciding which words to block.

Physical activity
Doesn't have to be anything especially strenuous. It can be anything from a bout of tickling (which you can do without actually having to get up yourself) to a fully organized game of football in the park. If you're planning the latter, though, be aware that your pre-schoolers will flout the offside rule about once a minute, and will do more protesting to the referee than the players in the average World Cup match could ever dream of. It's up to you whether you go as far as actually yellow carding them.

All of this is linked inextricably to their mental development. Let's be honest, your kids will take their cue from you. And you know what they'll do if a blank-faced parent is slouching on the sofa watching TV and belching, with bag of crisps nearby and four-pack of lager resting on a beer-gut. (They'll say, 'Budge up, Mum, make room for me.')

Chapter 33
Word Up

According to the US Department of Education, about *40%* of fourth-graders (age 9 to 10) can't read or understand a paragraph from a simple children's book.

Libraries are free. Maybe this needs to be said – unless people use their local libraries, they will wither and die.

You may recall the children's library you went to when you were little, and be stuck with a mental image of a dark, forbidding place staffed by a dragon in horn-rimmed spectacles who would briskly take your ticket and insert the little yellow slips showing which books you had borrowed. You may remember it as a place where you had to walk on tiptoe and there was always someone ready to turn round and go 'Sssh!' if you so much as breathed.

It's not like that any more. At least, not much.

Libraries are falling over themselves to get young children to use them. They even try and get babies coming in. Children's libraries, far from being dusty places where books are held in a mausoleum-like hush, punctuated only by the *ker-CHUNK* of the date stamp, seem more like nurseries and playgroups these days. They have reading tables, displays, Internet stations, comfortable sofas and even squashy cushions for little ones to sprawl on while reading. And why not? Anything that sends out the right message – that reading is (a) fun and (b) for everybody – can only be a good thing. (You see? I'm not always a reactionary old curmudgeon.)

You can also get children's books very cheaply from second-hand shops, fairs and toy sales. There's absolutely no need to buy everything new.

The book tower

They're never too young to start reading. Even when babies are more interested in chewing the crunchy cloth corners of the pages, it's important for them to *see* a book, to feel one, to turn the pages over and look at the pictures. When they come to identify letters and words later on, half the job will be done. There are books which double up as rattles, books which feature touchy-feely pages, plastic books which float in the bath and books which are carried in teddies' backpacks. It surely won't be long before you can get ultrasound books for your 20-week-old foetus to enjoy at his scan. (My idea. I should patent it.)

We're all advised to read to our children every day – at bedtime is a good option. If you can, put some 'expression' into it. No need to try to sound like Kenneth Branagh doing *Hamlet*, but if you can provide varying inflexion and silly voices, you're there.

There are some brilliant books out there for under-5s, and there are also some dreadful ones. You'll no doubt discover a lot for yourself. It sounds obvious, but in the early stages you should look out for books with bold lettering and clear pictures, and nothing too complicated. Some books which are meant to be for young toddlers make the mistake of having text in small fonts and pictures with too much going on. See Appendix 2 for some recommendations.

Stripped to the essentials

And what about that other staple of children's reading, the

comic? If you go into a newsagent's looking for a comic like the sort you used to read as a child – printed on newspaper and featuring up to twenty different one-page stories with lots of speech balloons to read – you may be sorely disappointed. Let's have a quick reminder of the kind of thing we mean.

The Beano: the classic one, pretty much unchanged down the years, and fronted as ever by Dennis The Menace and Gnasher. Somewhere, I still have a Dennis The Menace fan club badge and wallet. Also featured Minnie the Minx and the Bash Street Kids. It was corny, but pretty much always laugh-out-loud funny.

TV Comic: featured comic strip instalments of various TV shows such as *The Pink Panther*, *Charlie's Angels*, *Doctor Who* and *Top Cat*. However, many of them were oddly transposed into weird settings, e.g. Barney Bear, far from living in his usual log cabin in the mountains, became a Richard Briers-like dweller of suburbia, borrowing cups of sugar from his neighbour Moose (I'm not making this up) and getting embroiled in domestic crises. With hilarious consequences. Meanwhile, many of its other strips appeared, disappointingly, never to have been on television at all: 'Mighty Moth' or 'TV Terrors', anyone? And not forgetting 'The Kicktail Kid' (featuring Buzz Blaze and his incredible space-age skateboard), which would have blown the special effects budget of any company producing it as a regular series. Yes, it was a 'TV' comic in a very loose sense, but it was still good wholesome fun. In the late seventies, it merged with teen comic *Target*, and started to feature hard-hitting tales from cop shows like *Kojak*. The shark, I feel, was clearly jumped at this point.

The Eagle: re-launched in the 1980s for a new generation. I got the first new issue with its 'Free Space Spinner'. Dan Dare, Pilot of the Future, was still there as he had been in the 1950s, only this was Dan, grandson of Dan. (Whether the Mekon was also the grandson of the original Mekon is not recorded. I don't suppose it matters.) It also had photo stories, only not soppy romantic ones: the most memorable featured the scary Doom-lord, a skull-faced creature whose existence was uncovered by investigative reporter Howard Harvey who, shockingly, bought the farm from a lethal virus at the end. You didn't get that kind of stuff in *The Beano*.

Whizzer & Chips: the original concept of two rival comics in one. *Whizzer* was the one on the outside, while *Chips* nestled inside. Each one had its own 'editor' – Sid for *Whizzer*, Shiner for *Chips* – and kids were invited to choose their allegiance, either 'Whizz-Kid' or 'Chip-ito'. The rivalry was understood but never really explained.

You won't find that range these days. More often than not, children's comics are about twelve pages long at most and are little more than promotional catalogues for a TV programme and/or range of toys. These comics seem to be put together by trainee editorial staff straight out of college, who not only despise children but have never actually met any beyond their cousin's small nephew who they think smells of poo and half-eaten crisps.

There will be a 'free gift' stuck to the front, which will almost always (a) tear the cover in two when you try to remove it and (b) be unremittingly rubbish. What possible use can your child have for a plastic whistle, a doll-sized plastic 'guitar' with three nylon strings which doesn't even make a proper sound, or a pathetic 'spinner' or similar object?

About five or six pages will be taken up with supposedly 'educational' ballast in order to sell the publication to more sceptical middle-class parents. These include 'colouring activities' (a line drawing of Noddy! Woo-hoo, I wonder how long it took you to make that), join-the-dots, simple maze puzzles, etc. Some of them even have patronizing little pointers at the top of the page telling you which areas of the Key Stage One curriculum your child will be covering by doing this. Excuse me, you find yourself asking, but what is this, a school textbook? Whatever happened to reading comics for *fun*? And anyway, surely nothing is more educational than good, honest reading? Call me old-fashioned (and if you've got this far without flinging the book across the room in disgust, you almost certainly will do), but I think a comic can't go wrong by packing itself full of good, solid stories with lots of corny jokes.

Each comic used to have its own annual, and you could guarantee it would be a bumper, hardback version of the comic, sometimes with reprinted strips but, if you were lucky, with a whole wad of new ones. These days, children's annuals still thrive, but, depressingly, under more 'marketable' banners like the monikers of David Beckham and Barbie and the ubiquitous Tweenies. Naturally, they call this progress.

In the final assessment, while there's never been a healthier time for children's books, today's comics just aren't worth it. There is the odd good thing in them, but for the price you are really better off buying a decent picture book instead. (Or getting hold of some reprints of *The Beano*.)

Chapter 34
Kill Your Television

Average amount of TV watched per day by 5-year-olds:
4 hours
Proportion of under-3s with a TV in their bedroom: *42%*
Proportion of TV containing 'psychologically harmful' violence,
according to a study funded by the cable television industry:
57%

Why don't you ...?

TV is evil, right? TV is the bogeyman, the scourge of our time. It's the hypnotic box of tricks in the corner, turning our kids into a generation of passive zombies, unable to read, unable to think for themselves. Its pernicious images are slowly making them violent criminals and psychopaths.

Well, no.

Let's be realistic. Television is as varied as literature. The best children's television can be as fulfilling and as educational as the best books. The worst children's television exists only to promote ranges of small and expensive plastic figures (each sold separately) and is not worth bothering with at all.

Take the best-known global brand of TV, for example – the BBC. Their CBeebies channel has an excellent range of programmes unsullied by commercial breaks, both on terrestrial and digital/satellite, and they also promote the joys of reading quite heavily. All right, so they are no slackers when it comes to merchandising spin-offs, but it's usually done in a tasteful way and you don't *have* to buy *Bob The Builder* hats or *Fimbles* toothbrush-holders to enjoy the programmes.

Why not think of TV as a privilege, rather than a right? Then use it like chocolate, sweets or any other special treat. To ban the box entirely is probably impractical, and also means your children missing out on a whole range of cultural references and potential learning experiences – but there are ways to manage their viewing without exposing them to product placement.

Living in a box
Researchers on the BBC documentary *Child Of Our Time* looked into the effects of violence by seeing if watching violent images made children want to punch a man-sized rubber doll. Interesting that the doll rather resembled Mr Blobby, which perhaps gave an unfair bias to the experiment. After all, it should be in the genes of all children to want to punch Mr Blobby.

The same TV programme asserted that the average five-year-old watches four hours of television a day during the week, and more at weekends. Four hours! That's an impressive feat of viewing. Thinking of my own little telly addicts, that would mean the whole of *Stuart Little*, plus *Chitty Chitty Bang Bang* and a couple of episodes of *Bagpuss* and *The Koala Brothers*, with room to slot some *Pingu* in afterwards. I think I'd be ready to go out and punch a Mr Blobby doll after that.

Of course, they don't *have* to watch their four hours a day. It's not a quota. And like any statistical average, it's useless without knowing how it was arrived at. (Is this figure a mean, a median or a mode? What's the distribution curve like?) You could try letting your children, as soon as they are old enough, decide what their three or four favourite programmes are going to be and highlighting them in the paper or TV guide. It's then up to you to ensure that the television is turned on at the start of these, and off at the end.

Another study, published in April 2005 in the US journal *Archives of Pediatrics & Adolescent Medicine*, asserted that children who watch a lot of TV are more likely to become school bullies. Significantly, though, the research looked only at the time spent watching television and not the content of programmes – a failing which, by the researchers' own admission, rendered the results 'incomplete'. So the kids in the sample could have been watching hours of slice-and-dice anime, or they could have been stuck in front of the Discovery Channel for hours. Nobody knows.

The fact is, if your children are watching unsuitable stuff, it's not their fault, or the fault of the programme-makers. *It's yours.* Use a bit of common sense. A film called *Dragonslayer* is likely to feature a bit of sword-wielding and fake blood, while the chances are that *Homicide Squad* will show the odd drug dealer getting shot. It's not rocket science. If you don't want your kids to watch it, either make sure they're in bed or turn off the TV. It has an off switch. Use it wisely.

In any case, those findings quoted above were countered by the Centre for the Study of Popular Television at Syracuse University, which argued that the link was difficult to measure, and that any 'passive, isolationist behaviour that lasts for hours' could also lead to aggressiveness. So there you have it – TV *itself* may not be at fault, but rather the approach to child rearing which leaves children unstimulated. Interesting stuff.

The same charge, of course, is often levelled at video games, despite the fact that the evidence is inconclusive at best, some researchers having found that playing PlayStation games improved some young subjects' reactions and hand–eye coordination. There's no reason to doubt this, but nor is there any reason to doubt that it also puts a strain on their eyes, makes them tired and irritable and deprives them of more interactive pleasures like – well, like reading, for example.

If you believe everything you read, today's kids never go out, have never seen a vegetable, behave like pint-sized psychopaths and can't make their own entertainment. They exist on a diet of Coke and Turkey Twizzlers, while violent TV and video games mean they will be turned into numb-brained maniacs by the time they reach adulthood. Well, you may have played Pac-Man for hours on end as a child, but did you spend your twenties gliding around in dark rooms and swallowing pills to the accompaniment of weirdly repetitive electronic music? ... Actually, don't answer that.

Thing is, you can probably recall a time when there wasn't anything on TV during the day. There used to be something called *Closedown*. In the middle of the day! *Closedown*! Can you imagine that now? People would be running into the streets and staring at the skies. Yes, it's hard to imagine it now, but once upon a time, there were far fewer channels and they showed all their best-known programmes in the evenings. Television watching was something you did when the sun went down.[1] The old brown TV set hummed as it warmed up (who calls them TV *sets* nowadays?), smelling of heat and dust and wood. And, with a whine just on the edge of your hearing and which sometimes tingled on your teeth, the little white dot blossomed into a black-and-white picture as the darkness gathered outside. The whole experience had a hushed, reverential quality.

In the daytime it sat silently, waiting. It wasn't filled with bouncy weather girls, confessionals, magazine shows and discussion

---

1 Breakfast television, indeed any kind of daytime television at all, was still thought a decadent invention in the early 1980s, and some people simply refused to watch it.

bonanzas. We're talking as recently as the mid-1980s. You would turn on the television in the morning and – after waiting a few minutes for the thing to warm up – be greeted by a still frame of a girl playing an interminable game of noughts-and-crosses with a sinister clown, surrounded by geometric doodles in different kinds of shading. Can you imagine that now? In an era where we have entire channels devoted to country music, auctions of Argos jewellery and Rebecca Loos's Celebrity Enema? (And you tell that to the kids today, etc., etc …)

Even so – reality check. The cynical part of me wants to say that the golden days of classic BBC shows like *Bagpuss* and *Mr Benn* are long gone and that the TV our children will watch is an anodyne diet of rubbish produced by idiots and focus groups. Sadly, I can't, because the majority of today's pre-school TV – at least, the stuff put out by the esteemed Corporation – is absolutely brilliant.

Of course, some of it will drive you mad. The very first time you watch *Tweenies*, you may panic and think that somebody has laced your morning cup of tea with hallucinogenic drugs. The Tweenies are trapped like bees in a jar, caught in a chronic hysteresis; they are forever condemned to act out their nursery lives, to live their Orwellian hell within Aristotelean parameters for the entertainment of future generations. You'll find yourself wondering what children's TV's most obviously gay characters, PC Plum and Archie the Inventor from *Balamory*, get up to when the cameras aren't there. And above all, you start to reflect that it was never like this with *Ivor The Engine*.

Occasionally the odd commercial channel will slip through the net – Five's early morning re-runs of *Old Bear Stories* and *Noddy* were our Achilles heel – and you'll be forced to endure the adverts, which will baffle you even more efficiently. Most of the stuff advertised will be completely beyond your radar. What *are* those plastic things? How do they clip together, and why? Is that green stuff a kind of plasticine, or is it for eating? And let me get this right – that's Barbie, not being Barbie but somehow re-invented as a fairy in some sort of fantasy bonanza? Sorry, which planet am I on? I need my coffee.

And is it just me, or does the voice which says, 'Time for Teletubbies! Time for Teletubbies!' sound exactly like the Prime Minister, Tony Blair?

But if you do like those old, half-remembered 70s shows mentioned above, you can catch them after the kids have gone to bed – at the time of writing, the Nick Junior channel is repeating them in nostalgia-friendly slots in the late evening.

The sun always shines on TV
The one really sad thing about today's TV is this: the pubs and bars of the future will not be full of your children having 'Do you remember …?' conversations.

Many a student party in the late eighties was kept zipping along by alcohol-fuelled impressions of the Soup Dragon and people's desperate attempts to remember the name of the tortoise in *Pipkins*. But in 2022, nobody's going to be sitting there scratching their head over a pint of cheap Student Union beer and trying to remember what that old show was with the deserted library, and the clock whose hands went round and round until midnight. In the unlikely event that nobody has the DVD (or equivalent), someone will just be able to flip open their watch-mobile-computer-wi-fi-link, search for it on the Internet (or equivalent) and project a pin-sharp hologram image of *Storymakers* – for that's what it is – into the middle of the table (or equivalent) within seconds. They'll probably be able to download a bit-torrent of the entire series to watch that night in a cloud of green smoke, while debating with their online course-mates in Wyoming and Tasmania as to whether it ever 'jumped the shark'.

We who grew up in the 1970s and 1980s are the first and last generation to get our memories re-packaged and sold to us again via cable and DVD, because we're the generation who fell through the technology gap – that period in between the novelty of colour TV and the advent of home video. For about fifteen years, everything we watched just floated out into the ether and kept on going, with nothing there to capture it. It's all still heading out there – crackly old episodes of *Basil Brush* and *The Tomorrow People*, zooming off into space to be intercepted by the puzzled denizens of Alpha Centauri.

Children of the nineties and the zeroes can recover their memories instantly. The idea of *not* being able to watch a programme on video whenever you like is an utterly bizarre one to my small daughter. A child who is into, say, *Clifford The Big Red Dog* will probably not only watch the show but also own the books, the DVDs and the interactive CD, and will be a regular visitor to the BBC website. And you'll be amazed how many 3- and 4-year-olds, especially those who attend nursery school, can operate a mouse and navigate their way round a few simple icons.

Get used to it. This is the future.

It's not something which should make us throw our hands up in horror, railing at the passing of youthful innocence. On the contrary, it's a positive step. This is not the 1980s any more, thank goodness, and whatever the digital Luddites may think, interactive processes and multimedia are the way forward. If you want to deprive your children of those aspects of their education and entertainment, it's your loss – and it will be theirs.

Chapter 35
Would I Lie to You?

myth *n.* **1.** a traditional narrative usually involving supernatural or imaginary persons. **2.** a widely held but false notion. **3.** a fictitious person, thing or idea.

ritten and televised fictions aside, there are some other things you'll need to tell your children about in the interests of smooth running fatherhood, even though they won't necessarily be true.

1 The tooth fairy

This is the best one of all, you think. If you can convince your children of the existence of a kindly, nocturnal spirit who will remove ugly stumps of molar and replace them with shiny 50p pieces (or whatever the going rate is), then they'll believe anything.

In truth, of course, the kids are no fools. They have worked it out long ago and keep putting the teeth there because they know you'll keep bringing the cash. If they start trying surgical extraction of healthy teeth with pliers, then perhaps you could think about upping their pocket money.

A friend of mine was a volunteer for a charity delivering lunches to old people's homes, and used to take her four-year-old daughter on her afternoon rounds. The little girl was always intrigued by the various trappings of old age, especially the canes, walking frames and wheelchairs. One day, my friend found her daughter staring at a pair of false teeth soaking in a glass. As Mum braced herself for the inevitable barrage of questions, the little girl turned and whispered, 'Mummy! Look! The tooth fairy won't believe this!'

2 Father Christmas

On the face of it, this is the most implausible one of all. An old bloke in a red suit, carrying a sack full of presents, who heaves his portly frame down the chimney (and, presumably, through whatever heating arrangement you have there) in order to secrete the bounty in carefully arranged stockings? You couldn't make it up. Well, actually, someone did. And it's passed down from generation to generation.

Don't you find it somewhat surreal when you are queuing for an hour in a hot and crowded shopping mall, surrounded by screaming kids, just so that your child can go into a tacky polystyrene cave to see a funny old man in a big beard and tell him what she wants for Christmas? You spend all year telling your children not to go near strange old men, and then you take them to sit on the knee of one. Hmm. You then have to go along with the fiction that there is only one real Father Christmas and that all the others are 'helpers', which is really the point at which you should stop digging.

You're not always sure of the point at which your children work it out. When we had our fireplace ripped out and had a hole in the living room wall for a few weeks before the new one arrived, Darling Daughter got very suspicious. She would poke her little nose up into the sooty recesses and ask doubtfully, 'Does Father Christmas *really* come down there?' and 'What will he do when the new fireplace goes in?' Damn education.

But at least when they do finally get it, you haven't got to go through that annual palaver with the half-munched carrot, the mince pie crumbs and the empty sherry glass any more. It can only be a blessing.

3 Ogres and beasties

They live under the bed, allegedly. Best to knock this one on the head straight away. Best way to do it is to take the child on a voyage of exploration under said bed, and show him that the recesses contain nothing scarier than lost socks, piles of fluff and a game of Frustration with half the pieces missing. All of which is pretty horrible, but not quite in the same league as a lurking golem.

4 'I'm right, because I say so/because I'm older.'

You can't see this one going down well on *Newsnight*:

'Minister, I'd like to know exactly *why* you insist that you won't have to raise taxes to provide these new public services, when it's patently obvious that you will.'

'Now listen, Jeremy, I'm seven-and-a-half years older than you, and by the time you get to my age, you'll understand. Now drink your milk and go to bed '

5 The wind changing

There is no scientific evidence that a sudden change in wind direction will result in a comedy rictus being permanently affixed upon the child's face. However, your mum and dad probably said it to you, and so it behoves you to continue an important tradition.

6 Fair play

'It's not fair!' You can respond to this in a number of ways. 'Life's not fair' is one of the most popular. People often realize this at around the age of about 25, when they look at their horrible flat and their horrible job, and log on to Friends Reunited only to find out that Basher Barnes – that layabout from their class whose only goal in life was to extract dinner-money with menaces – is now running his own business and has a lovely house in the commuter-belt. So, the sooner you establish that there is no correlation between effort and reward, the better equipped your child will be for the real world.

7 God
This is a difficult call, not least because obviously lots of people genuinely do believe in this one and I've no desire to offend them here. Most children will, for some reason, probably picture God as a white-haired, white-bearded old man sitting on a cloud, swathed in a long cape or cloak and surrounded by attendant angels. One or two will have a more abstract concept, and one or two will be adamant that they don't believe in him at all. Up to you where you take this. Be prepared for difficult questions about resurrection, tsunamis, Ethiopia and why they didn't get an Xbox when they prayed for it. (And, when they've done their research, that whole where-the-hell-did-Cain's-wife-come-from thing and numerous other inconsistencies.)

8 Death
Some people swear by pets as the best way to introduce children to this concept. Depending on what you have, though, the time you have before confronting the subject will vary. Goldfish – no problem, they'll soon oblige. Cat or dog – traffic permitting, you ought to get a good few years' play out of it before the difficult issue is raised. And if you own a tortoise, you may not be getting the spade out until your children have kids of their own.

And finally ...
Top Difficult Questions (without suggested answers – I'm sure you can think of your own):

- 'Where did I come from?'
- 'Will you still love me when I'm big?'
- 'Will I still remember you when I'm dead?'
- 'Why has that lady got a beard?'
- 'Why doesn't glue stick to the inside of the bottle?'
- 'Why is the sky round?'
- 'Why do you have to go to work?'
- 'What are that man and lady doing on the television?'
- 'What's sex?'
- 'Why is water wet?'
- 'Why?'

Interlude: Conversations With My Daughter (2)

'You know, I sometimes can't believe we made you.'
'No, Daddy. God made me.'
'Rrrright ... Do you know who God is?'
'He lives in a place ... a looooong way away.'
'And what's it called?'
'Jamaica.'

Chapter 36
Solitude Standing

Your search – parent + 'time alone' – did not match any documents.
Google, 2005

The Not-We

Yes, them again. Do try, however hard it is, to stay in touch with your childless friends, especially the single ones. They will keep you grounded and give you topics of conversation other than those relating to your children. They may even provide you with hours of entertaining gossip. Think about it – who are the people you know with the most interesting love lives? (No, I'm sorry, the cast of *Desperate Housewives* does not count.)

And they make great substitute uncles and aunts, which is always useful if – as is increasingly the case these days – your biological family is (a) spread around the country, (b) likely to introduce an element of competition with their own children, or (c) annoying. Be prepared to field all those strange questions and comments from the childless, though.

The problem is, of course, that you will start to feel you have very little in common with them. The conversation may end up going something like this:

Non-Dad: Chelsea are doing well, aren't they?
Dad: Oh. Yeah. Um, I only saw half of it, actually. I was upstairs giving Rosie her bath and Calpol. And then Jessica asked for some water and a hug, and then I ended up having to talk to her for ages, and then I went for a lie down and woke up at midnight.

Non-Dad: … Bath and what?

Dad: Calpol. It's … sort of paracetamol stuff. For kids.

Non-Dad: Oh, right … I was listening to the new Cold-play album the other day. It's pretty good. Amazing that they've conquered the US charts now. They're the first to go straight into the Top 10 since the Beatles.

Dad: I've … not heard it.

Non-Dad: I'll burn you a copy off.

Dad: Thanks. Probably won't have time to listen to it for a while. Jessica screams the place down if we put anything other than her stuff on the stereo. Her behaviour's getting out of control, actually. We were seriously thinking of getting in touch with a child psychologist.

Non-Dad: Rrrright … Hey, that new Ridley Scott film looks good. Do you want to go and see it?

Dad: Depends if we can get a babysitter. And Rosie's being really clingy right now; she hates it if she finds out I'm going out and she's left with Mummy. Tonight she hung on to my leg and wouldn't let go. I bet she screamed the place down after I'd gone.

Non-Dad: Oh well … Time for another one?

Dad: I'd better not, actually. I'm really shattered.

Non-Dad: Lightweight.

Another country

You gradually start to realize that life goes on for your single friends and your non-parent couple friends, all of whom have other things to occupy them. Some of these activities don't sit very well with your life as a parent. Or do they?

- *Clubbing*: Hmmm. Loud noise, thudding electronic music, sleep deprivation, wandering around in a dazed state of bewilderment … sorry, but can't I get all that at home? And without paying a small fortune for a bottle of water?

- *Art exhibitions*: Yup, I'm used to looking at funny splodges and not knowing which way up they are meant to go. Old tin cans stuck together and sprayed green? Get them every day from nursery, mate. Stick your Turner Prize where the sun don't shine.
- *Cinema*: Sorry, you mean films *exist* without brightly animated characters talking in silly voices, wisecracking and saving the planet? Okay, I'd really love to come and see the latest French arthouse epic in which four good-looking intellectuals walk around Montmartre drinking, smoking, deciding which combination of them is going to sleep together and discussing what Roland Barthes would have to say on the matter. For three hours. But frankly, my bed calls.
- *Sport*: No need to go along to a stadium and support your local team. You can get the same rollercoaster of emotion from watching your little ones play, when they are old enough. Why pay good money to watch highly paid idiots kicking a ball around a muddy field, sulking, arguing with the officials and provoking unrest among the spectators when you can enrol your offspring in their local club and get it all for nothing? And you have the muddy kit to wash at the end of the weekend too.
- *All-night binge drinking*: Let me get this straight. You have a chance to have an uninterrupted night to yourself and you *don't* want to spend it sleeping? Are you sure you are quite sane?
- *Drugs*: If I want to spend time with someone who is hyperactive, strident and over-affectionate, while talking repetitious rubbish and thinking they are the centre of the universe, then I'll go and play with my two-year-old.

Chapter 37
A Design For Life

WARNING: chapter contains moderate emotional intensity and scenes of mild peril. May be unsuitable for parents of a nervous disposition.

nd so it's here. It will creep up on you like a slinky cat, or a cloudy day. School is a major watershed – it's the time when you finally feel you no longer have just a little boy or girl, but a fully-fledged child. It's time to get serious about uniforms, timetables and packed lunches. And sadly, in this day and age, it is time to get cut-throat.

Days like crazy paving

Education is marketed as a commodity like any other, and you may have been led to believe you are entitled to something called 'parental choice'. Excuse me while I stop to laugh hysterically. 'Choice' makes it sound as if selecting your child's first school is a process akin to deciding which variety of cereal to buy for them, or which brand of beans. *Nothing could be further from the truth*. Parental 'choice' is, by and large, a myth designed to make parents believe they have more influence than they actually do. In practice, most parents will end up sending their child to whichever school is reasonably near and has available places. This is equally true whether you live in an urban or a rural area.

Even those in power admit it's true:

'In reality, there is no parental choice. All the better schools end up being oversubscribed by parents exercising their choice for that school, so it is the school that ends up choosing the pupil, not the parent choosing the school.'

That's not a parent, a schoolteacher or an educationalist speaking. That's a quote from British MP Barry Gardiner (Labour member for Brent North). Food for thought.

The great escape

The so-called 'best' schools will be packed to the rafters with aspirational Jemimas and Jonnys. The little darlings may well be sweating in mobile classrooms holding 33 or more, and the teachers will be struggling to find enough resources to go round. Here is where you find the children of the hand-wringers – those who frown disapprovingly at the thought of private education, but who still make damn sure to jostle themselves into a decent catchment. They only come out in favour of the state system when they know Daisy's place at top-of-the-league-table St Eustacia's is safe. When faced with a less-than-stellar school, they are the first to throw their principles to the wind and go private.

Over on the other side of town are those who haven't any option but to send their children to whatever school they can find. Here's where you send your child if moving house wouldn't be an option or transport is limited. These school buildings – often decent enough – echo to the footsteps of ghosts, their empty desks sitting sadly, waiting in vain for pupils who will never come. Every year is a struggle for the head to justify the school's existence, let alone for the teachers to get on with teaching.

Out in the country, meanwhile, parents have only one realistic 'choice', and that's the local village school. That's assuming they can even get in, which is by no means guaranteed. Of course, there are those for whom this isn't good enough, and who will get the car out every day to do a five-mile school run in their children's best interests. They ignore the fact that the local school might actually benefit from their influence.

Along with sex, politics and your bank balance, schools should be a taboo subject with your friends, your colleagues and with people you meet at parties. It is (a) deeply boring for everyone else and (b) likely to lead to the following scenario:

1st Dad: So what are you doing about schools?
2nd Dad: Oh, we're going private, of *course*. There's no way we'd ever contemplate sending Harry to that hellhole, St Nigel's. Have you *seen* the place? The pupils are thugs and they get horrendous exam results ... Where are yours going?
1st Dad: St Nigel's.

Class war

Selection is alive and well. When middle-class parents talk about a 'good' school, they don't really mean the one where their child will get the best education, or meet the broadest range of people, or have access to the best educational and sporting facilities. They mean a school where little Raphael or little Petrina won't have to meet any children from the poorer areas, or anybody else who might – horrors! – speak with a working-class accent.

The richest and the poshest will already have withdrawn from the state system, meaning that it's only for the poorer and the principled. Some argue that those who can afford private education (and health) are doing society a moral service by using this resource, as it means they leave more state-funded resources to go round for everybody else. I offer this viewpoint without comment.

And catchments inevitably acquire a character – they either serve leafy suburban areas, or areas of 'traditional' housing, or quaint villages, or council estates (social housing). *It's still selection*. Only this time it's selection by mortgage, rather than by academic ability. The only truly *comprehensive* system would be one which put all children from the area into a big hat – or a computer program simulating this – and distributing them around all the available schools regardless of area and 'reputation'. Of course, this won't ever happen. For one thing, it would create a traffic nightmare. For another, it would cause estate agents to have heart attacks. And so we are left with a flawed system where parents treat the school league tables as if they were some oracle of truth. A system where 'good' schools, both primary and secondary, are largely nothing more than self-fulfilling prophecies. And one where those evil estate agents, rubbing their hands with glee, are the only real winners.

Want the proof? Have a look at your league tables. Go on, you can stomach it. You'll find them on the Internet. Now compare the house prices in those areas. Yes, it's not rocket science (or as they say at NASA, 'It won't need a Tiger Team'). The insidious, hate-generating league tables largely show you one thing, and one thing alone – namely, a rough idea of the socio-economic background of the catchment.

Do not, whatever you do, be misled into thinking that these statistics are somehow illustrative of the standard of teaching to be found in a school. Some of our most passionate and dedicated teachers can be found in the 'worst' schools in the country, while some of the laziest and most complacent will coast in the 'best'.

Hobson's choice
Factors sometimes taken into account with school allocation are siblings at the school, distance (for some urban schools, you

practically have to be overlooking the playground), parental preference (for what it's worth – usually nothing) and any rules about maximum class sizes. If you are intent on trying to make a 'choice' rather than simply sending your child to the school which is geographically nearest, here are a few pointers to get you started:

- Find out early about your local schools. When your child is three is about the right time to start making enquiries. (This is how it goes in theory – in practice, men start getting prospectuses and booking school visits as soon as the other half misses a period.)
- Generally, living in the catchment area for a particular primary school is *not enough* to guarantee a place. You need to express your preference for the local school and be living in the catchment too.
- Contact your local education department for further details. They won't come knocking on your door until it's too late – be proactive.

If you don't get the primary school you want, you can ask in writing for your case to be reconsidered, setting out your arguments in full. Don't expect miracles. If you are still turned down you can usually *appeal*. Don't get excited, though. It's a humiliating process and you'll be made to feel like the lowest link in the food chain. Noble talk of 'getting class sizes down' may sound good, but stop to think – this might mean *your* child being turned away because you are 31st on the list.

If you don't get your chosen school, make sure you stay on the waiting list, and keep yourself informed of progress. Under some authorities' guidelines, a family moving into the area could 'leapfrog' you if they live one house nearer. Check your own local council's policy.

A desperate venture

It's a horrendous nightmare, and you will become obsessed by it. You'll start to wonder if Mary and Joseph came all the way from Nazareth by donkey because Bethlehem Junior got better exam results and was a feeder for the sought-after Judea Grammar School, and if that grotty stable was all they could afford in the catchment.

Just in case you ever doubted how high passions can run, here are some of the measures parents might resort to (and have resorted to) in order to get their child into the catchment for a 'good' school. Be aware that, with some of these, you may well be on thin ice while carrying a heavy knapsack and wearing big skates:

- Moving house – sometimes parents even compromise on the house, being prepared to downsize for a 'better' area.
- Suddenly rediscovering the joys of religion to get into a faith school. This means braving the glares and taking your children to church every Sunday, just in order to secure that letter from the priest. It may mean thinking longingly of lunch in the pub during the mumblings of the *Te Deum Laudamus* (aka the Tedium Laudanum). It means trying not to swear at your little darlings as they hurdle the pews as if in training for the Olympics. This goes double for Catholic services, which seem to operate in a yet-to-be-scientifically-proven region of 'slow time'.
- Swapping addresses with a childless friend or a member of family (e.g. aunt or grandparent) who lives in the catchment. Prime them to field the inevitable phone calls, of course. This actually means lying, so it's not recommended.
- Buying a flat to rent in the catchment, and using that as the child's 'usual address'. You own the deeds, so it's not illegal, but you are pushing the boundaries here.

- And, most incredible of all, here's one I heard about recently. In 2004, the parents of a Birmingham 11-year-old had their child adopted by her aunt, who already had a child at a popular school, so as to increase the girl's chances of getting into the school on the 'siblings rule'. The head's comment was 'I have never heard of anyone going to these lengths.' (It didn't work, by the way.) It won't be long before we see children from shoddy catchment areas being auctioned on eBay for adoption by parents who live in areas at the top of the league tables. This may or may not be a joke.

One should add that schools are getting wise to the semi-legal dodges – some primary schools require prospective parents to come for an interview and may even visit them at home to confirm their addresses.

The fact that parents *are* prepared to go to the desperate lengths above, of course, is hardly a ringing endorsement of state education. So if you really aren't keen on the idea of school (and after all that, who could blame you?) then you have a legal right to educate your children at home. No special qualifications are needed and you don't need to follow a set curriculum. In England and Wales, have a look at **www.home-education.org.uk** for more information, or **www.schoolhouse.org.uk** if you are in Scotland. Try **http://homeschoolng.about.com** for general information, while at **http://www.midnightbeach.com/hs** you will find a page of home schooling resources.

Education, education ... yeah, whatever

Yes, it's terrible. These are the realities of 'choice' – which seems to be entrenching social exclusion and perpetuating divisiveness with each passing year. You can't help thinking it was all so much simpler in our day.

Good luck.

Chapter 38
I Wanna Be a Winner

'In the interests of fair education policy, under a Loony government all children will automatically be given full marks in their exams.'
From the Election Manifesto of the Monster Raving Loony
Party, 2005

Eggs and wooden spoons

At my school in the 1970s, we had a Sports Day at the end of every year. At that time, there was a fashion for putting schoolchildren into 'houses' for competition purposes, and so the school was divided up into four of these, colour coded with red, blue, green and yellow, and named after 20th century heroes (Bader, Bannister, Campbell and Hillary, for the record). So far, so good. I realize now how lucky our ordinary state primary was to have a big playing field all to itself – it's not something which many urban schools can boast.

Now, I wasn't great at sport, but I tried as hard as I could. You were competing for the honour of your house, after all, and competition was a *good* thing. It brought out the best in everyone. There were sack races, obstacle races, 'flat' races (simple mad-dash sprints), egg-and-spoon races … everything, really.

Our headmaster (essentially a caring man with a strong streak of totalitarianism, as all good headmasters are) was very proud of it all. Hello, Mr H., in the unlikely event that you're reading this. Rest assured that I'll never forget 'Clean Plate Day'. We may not have liked it at the time, but it got us all eating our cabbage. Jamie Oliver would have been proud.

The parents with their sideburns and dreadful glasses came along to applaud, the head announced the races and the results over a loudspeaker (usually inaudibly) and other teachers kept score with big white numbers on a giant blackboard at the end of the racetrack. At the end of the proceedings, the house with the most points would be adjudged the winner and a representative would be sent up to collect a trophy. This then led into a sequence of other presentations: prizes for achievements throughout the year in such things as swimming, football, chess and academic work. It was a fun day, it was all fair and good-natured and gave everyone a chance to win, while making it clear that only a few people would be the actual winners.

Some time in the last thirty years, this sort of thing went out of fashion. Now, children couldn't possibly be permitted to lose. Suddenly, expectations and assumptions were turned on their heads and we had Prizes For Everyone. All in all, you might say it was political correctness gone mad. (Sorry – political correctness experiencing mental health difficulties.)

You may wonder how this kind of thing is supposed to prepare kids for real life. Surely one of the most exciting things your child can do is to achieve a qualification or recognition through genuine hard work – and in something which he is *not naturally good at*.

I remember those school sports days fondly because my small contribution was helping my house to win. I also remember my sports teacher's grudging (and grunting) acknowledgement of me when, as a 14-year-old, I made the standard time in the 200 metres in athletics. And a friend of mine, a man with a Congratulatory First and a PhD from Oxford, is on record as saying that his Grade C in Art is the qualification he's most proud of – simply because, by his own admission, he draws like a monkey.

In the UK, a whole generation went on to secondary school with the idea that they weren't allowed to fail – and a new exam called the GCSE was brought in to reinforce this odd idea. Now you no longer actually had to do any work; you could have a certificate to show you'd got a Grade F, and that was as good as any other.

Every year, we see greater numbers of A and A* grades being awarded. Every year, there is a chorus of doubt from those who are highly dubious about these 'rising standards'. And every year, these doubts cause a backlash of outrage from those who are furious that we dare to impugn the hard work and the achievements of today's young people. But either (a) today's students are brighter and more hard-working than ever, or (b) the exams are easier.

And nobody ever stops to think about the reverse implications of (a) – namely, that those of us who went to school in the 1970s and 1980s must therefore be more stupid and lazy than today's young people. By logical extension, it also implies that our parents' generation wouldn't have known how to get to school and couldn't have told one end of a pencil from the other when they got there. You don't need GCSEs to realize how daft this is.[1]

The universal
The idea of expanded university places has been sold to people by dangling a carrot, namely the idea that graduate earnings

---

1   There is a possible compromise option – that today's students are more effectively taught to pass exams than we were – but it still doesn't fully explain the phenomenon.

add up to vastly more than those of non-graduates over a life-time – a notion which is surely 20 years out of date, as it's based on figures from a time when only a select few went to university.

Yes, we are supposed to believe that our children's generation will be better off because half of them are trotting off to read for daft-sounding degrees at even more ludicrous universities. Forgive me for being a little cynical. One might also wonder how on earth universities are going to accommodate these extra students, given that most Halls of Residence have waiting lists as it is. No doubt even more students will find themselves living in areas of cities which are not traditionally 'studenty', and pushing even more families – people like you and me – out of the housing market.

It's not more graduates we need – it's more skilled workers. If you've ever tried to get hold of a joiner to fit you some cupboards, or a plumber to fix your washing machine, or a builder to quote you on an extension, you may have come to the conclusion that we're somewhat lacking in dependable craftspeople. On the other hand, we already have more than enough people with 2.2s in Peace Studies and Aromatherapy from the University Of Central Bogshire (formerly Bogchester Polytechnic). And there are more people currently studying for UK degrees in Photography than there are photography-related jobs *in the entire European Union*.

But that's the thing – you're not allowed to suggest this any more, because it makes some people look like winners and others like losers. No matter that cabinet making and plumbing are hugely technical, respected and in-demand skills which can prove very lucrative after a few years. Never mind the fact that the former Chief Inspector of Schools, Chris Woodhead, has suggested that it's absurd to make non-academic kids feel like failures by putting them through academic exams and that more vocational courses need to be made available. Despite all that, many parents still want their kids to toddle off to a cardboard university to earn a rice-paper degree which will qualify them for precisely nothing. 'Social inclusion' isn't about shoving everyone into further and higher education – it's about giving everyone the chance to make the best of their skills, which may or may not be academic.

Some time in their life, *your children will fail*. It may be their driving test or a music exam. It may be at a university exam or a job interview. It may be a first experience of unrequited love. Whatever it is, you will want to be there for them. Nobody's saying you shouldn't encourage your children to aim high, to have ambition. But failure is part of the human condition – it's almost a human right. Teach children that they have the right to do anything, and they will grow up being suitable for nothing.

And if they ever came last in the egg-and-spoon race at their school Sports Day, they may understand this a whole lot better.

Chapter 39
Alphabet Street

y the time your child starts school they will also, with any luck, have learnt to master the *alphabet*. It's useful for you, as it can prove an effective mnemonic to remind you of what you may have learnt over the past five years. Here are the 26 key points of your dad experience, helpfully presented in A–Z format.

A is for ... Aaaaaaaaarrrgh!
You'll feel like saying it at least once. That's once a day, probably. Walk right down to the end of the garden (or the end of your street if that's not far enough) and get it out of your system.

B is for ... Babies
You will have started seeing them everywhere. They will all be perfectly nice, but nowhere near as beautiful as your own. And people who have them are your allies. For now. In five years' time, though, they will be your competitors for the places at the only decent primary school for miles around. Start the psychological warfare early.

C is for ... Carrying
When taking a child out, go everywhere armed with a little rucksack, packed with more stuff than you actually need (spare clothes, water, breadsticks/rusks, wipes, nappies, and so on). It will be worth it for the one time you do need it all. However, don't underestimate the toddler's potential as slave labour – fetching and carrying, answering the phone, etc. It'll come in handy when you have your second one. Stop laughing at the back.

D is for … Destitute
You no longer have any money. At least, none to spend on your-self. Just to remind you, the average cost of bringing up a child from birth to age five is thought to be £52,605. So I'd start saving now if I were you.

E is for … Entertainment
Swallow your pride and go to one of those horrible play-zone places. They can romp around in coloured plastic balls for an hour and you get to have a sit down and a cup of tea – maybe even read the paper if you're really well prepared. You can always tell Mum that you went to the park. Come on, Toddler's not going to tell on you, is she?

F is for … Fickleness
Especially true of little girls. One day, she will prefer Daddy. The next, she will prefer Mummy. You always seem to judge it wrongly. This will continue for about 20 years.

G is for … Gormless
You're standing in a shop or in the office and somebody asks you a perfectly normal question. It might be something like 'What time's that meeting?' or 'What's your name?' And for a moment you aren't quite sure what they mean. You suddenly realize it has happened – becoming a dad has taken your IQ down about 40 points. It's not just your hair that recedes. Will you ever get it back? Read Daniel Keyes' *Flowers For Algernon* and worry.

H is for … Hyperactive
Before you had children, you may have seen someone else's three-year-old careering around the lounge and smashing into the walls – and secretly thought to yourself, 'It's OK, mine won't

be like that. He's hyperactive.' You won't really have known what it meant, but it'll have sounded good. Also useful for excusing horrific actions on the part of a little terror. If a toddler hooligan has a little Burberry cap, a pierced ear and a football shirt and lives on a council estate, he's a thuggish little horror. If he's from a big house in a leafy suburb and dresses in Gap, he's got ADHD.

I is for ... Isolation
I would go out tonight, but I haven't got a stitch to wear. Actually, no – it's because there is a small screaming person upstairs and we don't have a babysitter. Will you ever get to have a social life beyond those snatched half-hours in the pub after work? Yes, probably, when they're about sixteen and can be left at home on their own. Up until then, you have to get used to the idea that you'll be having a lot of takeaways and evenings on the sofa. Because otherwise it means a babysitter (double the cost of your night out) or using family (double the preparation for your night out).

J is for ... Journalists
Every week, someone in the press will have a new opinion on child rearing. Whenever you see the latest round of 'Child-free versus Breeders' about to brew up in the dailies, it's very tempting just to put your feet up, crack open a beer and start chanting, 'Fight! Fight! Fight!'

K is for ... Kickabout
On Sunday mornings, the parks are full of men teaching little daughters in football shirts how to take corners and apply the offside rule. Just don't walk up to them and say, 'Wanted a boy, did you?'

L is for … Life
That which seems to be going on elsewhere, and which you don't think you will ever get to have again. Make yourself feel better by reading a miserable article by someone who desperately wants children. You'll also have read about these 'empty nester' people in their forties and fifties who are suddenly bereft because their children have left home. They are moaning because the house is suddenly *too quiet* and they have *lots of time to themselves*. You blink, read that again. Yes, that really is what they are moaning about. Maybe some sort of exchange scheme is in order?

M is for … Mum
For some reason, you and your wife will lose the ability to refer to one another by your first names. You know it's got serious when you start doing it when the kids have gone to bed. 'Would you like a cup of tea, Mum?' 'Go on then, Dad.'

N is for … Names
Have a look at an entertaining website called the 'Baby Name Wizard' at **www.babynamewizard.com** – click on its 'Name Voyager' icon, enter a particular name and a dynamic graph will plot the progress of its popularity over the last hundred years. Oddly compelling.

O is for … Onanism
Let's face it, you won't be getting much else while the baby's little. And it's the best way to reduce your chances of prostate cancer, so I'm told.

P is for … Poo
It only takes twenty minutes a day to wash a nappy, they say.

You, Dad, can do this mindless task. Alternatively, you can use disposables, and spend the time watching an extra episode of *Balamory* with Toddler, singing silly songs to Baby or doing the crossword. Or just having a nap.

Q is for ... Queen
Who wants to live forever? Don't stop me now, because I'm a good old-fashioned lover boy. On the other hand, I want to break free, I want to break free. It's a hard life and I'm under pressure. Save me, save me, save me, because I'm going slightly mad ... Yes, there's a song for every occasion. Lull your children to sleep with the gentle drumming of Roger Taylor and the restrained guitar lilt of Brian May. Well, it worked for mine. Remember: the show must go on.

R is for ... Rabbit
My daughter's favourite bedtime companion. Started out fluffy and white (he was sold as an Easter bunny, I believe) and now, after several washes, seems miraculously to be holding entropy at bay – in stark defiance of Maxwell's Second Law of Thermodynamics. If they're going to have a special teddy or other fluffy object, make it a washable one if you don't want a biohazard on your hands. Or worse, screaming and traumas when Mr Fluffy disintegrates in the boil-wash.

S is for ... Shopping
For some odd reason, baby food is always located on the aisle opposite what they euphemistically call 'Feminine Hygiene'. Men with trolleys usually hug the baby food side of the aisle, making it clear that they are here for the express and very masculine purpose of buying nourishment for the Fruit Of Their Loins, and that they have no interest in the tampons. 'There

may be men who enjoy browsing among the sanitary towels for nefarious purposes, possibly to chat up single mothers like that bloke in the Nick Hornby book,' your body language is saying, 'but I assure you I am not one of them.'

T is for ... Tantrums

A really good one takes practice. Wailing, foot stamping, screaming, tears – they all have to be applied in perfect symbiosis. You'll get the hang of it. But seriously – never underestimate the stamina and aggression of the toddler. You should develop a thick skin and some elementary martial arts skills. These can be achieved by (a) allowing your beloved to point out your shortcomings on a regular basis and (b) watching Bruce Lee films.

U is for ... Ultrasound

It was the first time you ever saw your little one. Remember? Doesn't it seem like an awfully long time ago? Like something that happened to somebody else – somebody who had more hair and slept a lot? Look at photos, and weep.

V is for ... Vegetables

Your child will object to these from quite an early age. It just always seems to happen, no matter how many good intentions you may have about bringing them up on home-grown courgettes and organic parsnips. The best way to get your child to eat vegetables is to lace things they like with them. We tried sneaking mashed swede in with a strawberry yoghurt once (result: Toddler's instant projectile expulsion of devilish mixture across table, floor and self) and slipping some finely grated carrot into the mashed potato (result: fingers crossed, still seems to be working). Wife wants to make sure she gets the credit for this idea. Duly done.

W is for ... Wipes

When your baby is very small, you'll find yourself using cotton wool and water for pretty much everything. After that, though, wipes come into play, and you may well find yourself concluding after a few weeks that they are the best invention to come out of the twentieth century after the flush lavatory and the Internet. You'll end up taking the little packets everywhere: the park, the pub, the playgroup, friends' houses. You can spot the supremely-organized parents, as they are the ones who will have a pop-up box (not just a packet) of wipes in every room. Trust me, they are vital even when your child is five. It will become second nature to you to reach for the wipes at the first sign of any dripping or dribbling – so much so that, at work, you will start looking round for them when somebody spills a drop of coffee in a meeting.

X is for ... Xylophones

Instruments of the devil. Don't buy them. Instruct your family not to buy them. They. Will. Drive. You. Mad.

Y is for ... Youth

That which has passed you by. You gaze in the mirror and are shocked to see that your reflection has been somehow usurped – there is a stranger gazing back at you, one who seems about five or even ten years older than they should. Attempt to recapture youth with occasional 'boys' nights out' (at which you feel like crawling into bed halfway through the second pint) and listening to eighties compilations at full volume.

Z is for ... Zzzzzzzzzzzz

Now excuse me while I have a little kip.

Chapter 40
There Is a Light That Never Goes Out

The 2005 conference of the Professional Association of Teachers was told:

'Poor parenting fosters lack of respect and no manners ... No wonder then that, having no guidelines, children enter education with limited knowledge about appropriate behaviour. Staff in education are expected to teach social skills which should have been learnt at home. They find themselves "policing" classes rather than teaching.'

Batteries not included

he one thing you will undoubtedly have come to realize is that children don't arrive with instructions on the box. It's diverting to imagine how these might read:

- You have chosen to purchase and install *Child 1.0*. The manufacturers are not responsible for any defects. Or maybe they are. Or perhaps it's Society. The jury's still out on that one, to be honest.
- Please note that the system will upgrade itself automatically, and that other features such as Tantrum 2.2, Mess (Beta Release) and Disobedience XP will install themselves randomly at some point over the next three years.
- This product will automatically *uninstall* the following files: nightsdownthepub.exe, quiet_lie-in.exe and luxury-purchases. exe.

- We recommend installing the background application program C:\RESIGNED-ACCEPTANCE. This will save a lot of confusion and disappointment with your product.
- Please note that *Child 1.0*, while a high-quality product, is also high maintenance. We recommend purchasing upgraded versions of Toys XP and Special Treats 7.0 on a regular basis. (However, users have reported problems using the files bribes.exe and threats.exe, so these are to be avoided.)
- Some users are concerned about extraneous features, especially the 'Are we there yet?' 'Why?' and 'I want' pop-ups. Unfortunately, these come as standard and are unable to be blocked.

Bad dad?

So what is a 'good' dad? Is it someone who is well-balanced at all times, calm and sane in the face of all adversity? A parent who produces a perfect child, well-scrubbed and well-dressed, who speaks respectfully at all times and never steps out of line? Or is it more likely to be a dad who knows his child's foibles and how to deal with them? (Some recent research suggests, for example, that girls like to be 'people-pleasers', and that they should be encouraged to take risks and to judge their own efforts rather than always to toe the line.)

The combination on which most people seem able to agree is that of love and discipline – the hardest mix to get right. There may be the odd day when you feel it's all too much, and there will always be times when you want to yell at them for spilling orange juice on your DVD collection. So, yes, they may sometimes be little blighters. But they are *your* little blighters. And most of the time, you will not be able to imagine – or want – life without them. It's impossible. It's like trying to imagine a world without sky, or music. Try to think of what your house was like before it echoed to the sounds of children's laughter. Can you even picture it?

The other key thing you feel is a strong, instinctive sense of protection. There is nothing like parenthood for making you feel simultaneously strong and fragile. You are the father, the guardian. At the same time, you feel as if the whole world has suddenly become dangerous. You want to cling on to your children, pull them away from cars, away from kerbsides, from dogs, from other people. Of course, you can't. There is no force field, no protective aura like the one which used to surround the children in the old Ready Brek adverts. You just have to do the best you can.

Bittersweet symphony

Yes, you will almost certainly feel that you've had a rapid learning curve as a father. You'll reach the point where you start to wonder what you talked about before you had children. And looking around at all the carefree twenty somethings who have suddenly materialized from nowhere, you start to marvel at how young and fresh they all look, and how free from woes.

But you'll also start to lose sight of whatever it was that made life so great before. The thought of being free to go out to pubs, clubs and restaurants without any responsibility for anyone but yourself will start to seem … immature, somehow. You'll look around at the young people buzzing about town with their trendy clothes, their unlined faces, convinced they have the weight of the world on them because they have fallen out with their girlfriend/boyfriend or their landlord has turned out to be a bit of a swine, and you'll think: you've got it all coming. I know a bit about life, now. This small person here in the pushchair has *taught* me something. And as they sashay past, yapping about the banalities of their life, they may cast a nervous glance at your child, possibly even tinged with disgust. But you don't care. Because you have evolved, and they have not. Your wheel has turned, and you are on a different ride.

In fact, it sometimes seems as if you are in a different world altogether. You can talk about anything and it just doesn't matter any more; you are oblivious to people looking at you as if you are mad. Shortly before her fifth birthday, Daughter and I had a conversation on the way to the bus stop about something called 'the children's sky'. It was based on her idea that there is one sky for adults and one for children, and that the one for children is higher up. Worryingly, it made a weird kind of sense at the time.

And here, just in case you have lost sight of why you embarked upon this journey in the first place, is a short list of several other things you can *only* do now that you have a child:

- See the sun rise. In summer.
- Be tired enough to get off to sleep at night without too much trouble.
- Play on swings and slides without getting suspicious looks.
- Buy videos/DVDs of the old TV programmes you used to love, on the grounds that they will be 'educational'.
- Have a small person looking up at you and nodding, wide-eyed, as you tell them something really exciting.
- Build sandcastles, complete with portcullis, driftwood draw-bridge, little flags and system of water channels feeding the moat. (All right, you could do this before, but it was never as satisfying.)
- Play football/cricket and not have to be very good.
- Have an excuse to buy toys at Christmas.

- Take it upon yourself to impart your wisdom and experience to someone who will listen without rolling their eyes (until they are about 11, anyway).
- Get Father's Day presents, especially home-made ones.
- Have someone spend an hour glueing bits of paper, feathers and glitter on to a card for you, just because they want to.
- Hear someone say 'I love you, Daddy.'

The ultimate salutary thought

Oh, and whatever they do, however they try your patience and make you grind your teeth, you'd better keep on the good side of them. After all, in a few decades' time, the wheel may have come full circle – and they could be the ones feeding you, putting you to bed and pushing you around in a chair.

Have fun. It's all worth it. Honest.

Appendix 1
Is There Something I Should Know?

lthough I don't wish to make this too much like a course book, I have found the following entertaining and/or interesting to some degree and I hope you will too.

Steve Biddulph, *Raising Boys* (Thorsons, 1998).

Rohan Candappa, *Autobiography of a One Year Old* (Ebury, 2000).

Arlene Eisenberg, Heidi E. Murkoff & Sandee E. Hathaway, *What To Expect: The First Year* (Simon & Schuster, 1993); *What To Expect: The Toddler Years* (Simon & Schuster, 1996).

Christopher Green, *New Toddler Taming* (Vermilion, 2001).

Patrick Hanks & Flavia Hodges, *A Dictionary of First Names* (Oxford University Press, 1990).

Dave Hill, *Dad's Life* (Headline, 2003).

Phil Hogan, *Parenting Made Difficult* (Piccadilly, 2002).

Charles Jennings, *Fathers' Race* (Little, Brown, 1999).

Libby Purves, *How Not To Be A Perfect Mother* (HarperCollins, 2004).

Ian Sansom, *The Truth About Babies From A–Z* (Granta, 2002).

Sarah Tucker, *Have Toddler Will Travel* (Hodder & Stoughton, 2002).

And here's a *highly selective list of websites*, chosen on the basis of being informative and user-friendly. See these sites as the starting points in each case – they will no doubt lead you on to plenty of others.

dadlands

Topic	Website address
Babies:	www.babyworld.co.uk
	www.howtoreadyourbaby.com
Baby names:	www.babynamewizard.com
Behaviour:	www.handbag.com/family/yourtoddler/tantrums
	www.practicalparent.org.uk/faq2.htm
Childcare:	www.childint.com
	www.ncma.org.uk
Children's books:	http://books.guardian.co.uk/childrenslibrary
	www.bookitfamilies.com
	www.cbuk.info
Children's Society:	www.the-childrens-society.org.uk
Education:	www.bbc.co.uk/schools/parents
	www.earlychildhood.com
Fathers (general issues):	www.dads-uk.co.uk
	www.fathers.com
	www.fathersforum.com
	www.fatherville.com
Fathers and daughters:	www.dadsanddaughters.org
Fathers and sons:	www.dfes.gov.uk/dadsandsons
Home dads:	www.homedad.org.uk
Home education:	http://homeschooling.about.com
	www.home-education.org.uk
	www.schoolhouse.org.uk
Internet chat safety:	www.bbc.co.uk/chatguide
Issues and campaigns for men:	www.coeffic.demon.co.uk/organiz.htm
Miscarriage support:	www.babyloss.com
	www.miscarriageassociation.org
Out and about:	http://travelwithkids.about.com/od/babiestips
	www.babycenter.com/expert/faq-babytravel.html
Parenting (general issues):	www.babycenter.com
	www.bbc.co.uk/parenting
	www.juniormagazine.co.uk
	www.parenting.org
	www.parents.com

Topic	Website address
Parties for children:	http://kids-party.com/partytips.htm
Pregnancy:	http://pregnancy.about.com/od/forfathersonly
	www.nctpregnancyandbabycare.com
Relationships:	www.bbc.co.uk/relationships/couples/life_newbaby.shtml
Restaurant recommendations:	www.forparentsbyparents.com/baby_feeding_restaurants.html
Safety:	www.capt.org.uk
	www.forparentsbyparents.com/info_safe_home.html
Single fathers:	www.singlefather.org
Sleep for babies:	www.babycentre.co.uk/sleep/
	www.theallineed.com/family/family-018.htm
Television:	www.abc.net.au/children
	www.bbc.co.uk/cbeebies
	www.kids-tv.co.uk
Toys and games:	http://childparenting.about.com/cs/toys/a/kidstoys.htm
	www.theukhighstreet.com/shops/toys
Working parents:	www.parentsatwork.org.uk
	www.workingparents.com

Appendix 2
Like a Child Again

his is just a very small selection of the books which have worked best with our children – other people's mileage will vary but, hey, it's my list.

- Eric Carle, *The Very Hungry Caterpillar* (Hamish Hamilton)
A simple, effective idea and a timeless classic. Get the sturdy board-book version. It won't take long before they are joining in.

- Michael Rosen & Helen Oxenbury, *We're Going On A Bear Hunt* (Walker Books)
Another one to get them joining in – lots of bouncing rhythm and silly sounds, and a lovely twist at the end.

- Eric Hill's *Spot* books (Frederick Warne) and
- Rod Campbell's *Dear Zoo* (Campbell Books)
Lift-the-flap books for young toddlers to get involved in.

- Emma Chichester Clark's *Blue Kangaroo* series (Collins)
Blue Kangaroo is a hero for our times. The favourite comforter of a precocious (but loveable) little madam called Lily, he is, variously, nudged out of bed by a menagerie of newbies, abandoned at the zoo and blamed for all of his young owner's misdemeanours – but still endures it all with loyalty and stoicism. He even undertakes a daring moonlit rescue mission. Lovely pictures and simple stories, probably best for girls aged 2–6.

- Julia Donaldson & Axel Scheffler, *The Gruffalo* (Macmillan)
In a deep, dark wood, a cunning mouse escapes several preda-

tors by pretending to be best mates with the fearsome Gruffalo – and then has to think quickly when he comes face-to-face with the beast himself. All told in rhyme, the story will quickly become a favourite. In the sequel, *The Gruffalo's Child*, the Gruffalo's firstborn ventures into the forest and encounters a big, terrifying mouse … or not? There's also a Gruffalo stage play and *The Gruffalo Songbook* … Expect the movie, CD-ROM and decorative tea towel before too long.

- Julia Donaldson & Axel Scheffler, *Room On The Broom* (Macmillan)

Another rhyming story from the Gruffalo creators, and this time it's about a witch. She's not a scary, cackling, warty witch, but a friendly one who just wants to get on with her job of flying round on her broomstick with her cat. She ends up having to pick up a number of passengers on the way – but the hangers-on turn out to be very useful when it comes to saving her from a fearsome dragon. Very funny, engagingly told and cleverly illustrated.

- The *Mr Men* and *Little Miss* books by the late Roger Hargreaves, latterly continued by his son Adam (Egmont)

You may remember these from your own childhood. The actual quality of the stories is variable, but everyone will have their favourite. I defy you not to decide which one your child most resembles.

- Jane Hissey's *Old Bear* books (Red Fox)

Or 'Playroom Uncovered', the first teddy bear docusoap. A band of cheerful and resourceful soft toys attempt airborne rescues from attics, stage exciting boat races, organize picnics, sports days and pantomimes, build snowmen and dragons, bake cakes and generally have a great time. Basically, they do all the stuff that your child wants to think her teddies get up to when her back is turned. Each character is brilliantly defined and the stories progress logically. Worth complementing these with the audio and video versions, both narrated by Anton Rodgers – the 20-minute, effects-laden seasonal extravaganza, *Little Bear's Christmas Star*, has become essential Christmas Eve viewing in our household.

- Dawn Apperley, *There's An Octopus Under My Bed* (Bloomsbury)
Molly's good at playing but not so good at clearing up. She can't work out how all her mess gets mysteriously tidied up when she is not looking. Very funny and cutely illustrated – and you're bound to empathize with the idea that children think there is a mysterious, invisible Mess Octopus.

- Kes Gray & Nick Sharratt, *Eat Your Peas* (Red Fox)
The first in a series featuring the irrepressibly mischievous Daisy, toddler terrorist. In this first outing, Daisy's mum offers a series of increasingly unlikely bribes in order to get the little minx to try her greens. Watch out for an ending of dubious moral resonance.

- Hilary Robinson & Nick Sharratt, *Mixed Up Fairy Tales* (Hodder)
The pages are segmented into four, so that random flap-turning will produce such surreal gems as, 'Goldilocks liked to nibble grass and dreamt about marrying a bowl of soup,' or 'Cinderella cried "Open Sesame!" and was put into a cooking pot to be turned into a troll.' Hours of fun – and thousands of possible combinations.

- Janet Lawson, *Audrey And Barbara* (Simon & Schuster)
A charmingly surreal story of a little girl and her laconic cat planning a trip to India in an old bathtub with pram-wheels. A lot is

conveyed in the minimal narration and detailed illustrations. It's implied that they have more adventures, but as yet I haven't been able to track any down.

- Angela McAllister & Jason Cockcroft, *Blue Rabbit* (Bloomsbury)

Neatly turns the 'lost toy' story on its head – Blue Rabbit becomes distressed when his Boy vanishes one day. The other toys try to help, but it seems he's gone for good. Don't worry, it's not *Bambi*. He's only gone on holiday, and there is a sweet reunion at the end.

And one to grow up with …

- J.R.R. Tolkien, *The Hobbit* (HarperCollins)

I've had a soft spot for this ever since I got it in my Christmas stocking in 1975. There are two generations (at least) for whom simply the names 'Rivendell' and 'Smaug' will release a Proustian flood of childhood memories, and we owe it to our children to continue the heritage. Much of the language and the plot will be beyond the average pre-schooler, but who cares? There's nothing wrong with reading them stuff which is above their level. The rhythm, atmosphere and verve of the writing will carry them along, and with any luck they will come back to it later when they are reading for themselves. *Your children need this book*. If they grow up without the Misty Mountains, Gollum and The Song About Gold ingrained into their psyche, they will be seriously impoverished. Don't listen to the politically correct do-gooders who whinge on about how Tolkien was unreconstructed in this, that or the other opinion and how children shouldn't be reading his reactionary stuff. They're just jealous because they could never write anything this good for kids.

Afterword
Put the Message in the Box

 'd be interested to hear your experiences of fatherhood, as well as comments on any of the issues raised in this book – you can send them to **dan80s@hotmail.com**.

I'll write back if you seem like a reasonable human being.